LeBron James

The King of the Game

D0937472

LeBron James

The King of the Game

Rick Leddy

Sole BOOKS

A special thank you to Yonatan, Yaron, and Guy Ginsberg.

Cover design: Omer Pikarski

Front cover picture: AP Photo/Tony Dejak
Back cover picture: Mark L. Baer, *USA TODAY* Sports

Series editor: Y Ginsberg
Proof editor: Michele Caterina
Page layout design: Lynn M. Snyder

Library of Congress Cataloging-in-Publication data available.

ISBN: 978-1-938591-25-9

Published by Sole Books, Beverly Hills, California

Printed in the United States of America
First edition March 2015

10987654321

www.solebooks.com

Sad Christmas

"Duck!" Little LeBron screamed as he rushed toward the basket. LeBron's mother, Gloria, smiled sadly. A tear was rolling down her cheek, but she couldn't help but smile. LeBron was having such a good time. Each time he yelled, "Dunk!" it sounded like he was shouting, "Duck!"

She was so happy and so sad at the same time. She wanted to pick up three-year-old LeBron, squeeze him hard, and never let him go, but she knew he would only want to wriggle free of her grasp, grab his toddler basketball, and yell, "Duck!" again, before tearing off toward the miniature basket to slam the ball through the hoop.

The living room in her mother's Hickory Street

home in Akron was in disarray; torn wrapping paper and toys were strewn about like a tornado had hit the inside of the house. Gloria didn't have much, but what she did have she showered on little Bron. As she watched her little boy approach the plastic hoop and slam the basketball over and over again, Gloria couldn't help but wonder at the tenacity of this toddler. He had a drive that made him want to repeat something until he was happy with the result.

Eddie Jackson, her boyfriend, sidled next to her as she watched LeBron.

"I never seen a kid that little able to do that." Eddie whispered.

Gloria looked up at Eddie and buried her head in his shoulder. The strain of the day was showing on her face.

"Why? Why didn't Mama ever tell us she was so sick?" she sobbed.

Eddie kissed her on the forehead. "I don't know, Glo. Your mama was so busy taking care of all of us that she didn't take time to look after herself."

Eddie was the one who had discovered Gloria's mother, LeBron's grandma, slumped on the kitchen floor at three o'clock that morning. And it was Eddie who had gathered Freda in his arms, gently rocking her back and forth, staying with her until the ambulance came.

Freda James had been the rock of the family. She was the one who looked after Gloria and her two brothers. It may not have been the best neighborhood in Akron, but the residents took pride in their houses and the house on Hickory Street was Freda's kingdom. It was Freda who made sure there was always a roof over her children's heads. When Gloria, who was only 16 years old, had LeBron, Freda took in her grandson without a complaint. She took care of him while Gloria went back to high school. He was a James and that was that. And she loved that little boy.

Eventually, she had even taken in Eddie, who was Gloria's boyfriend. With Freda, you didn't have to be family to be family. Family was just something that was waiting to happen. And now she was gone. Just like that. On this very Christmas morning.

"Look at Bron. So happy," Gloria said, wiping tears from her eyes.

Eddie wrapped his arm around her shoulder and gave it a squeeze. "You did that boy right. You gave Bron Christmas. I know how hard this is for you."

"Mama wouldn't have stood for nothing else," Gloria said. "I can just hear what she would've said if we canceled Christmas for that little boy."

LeBron ran up to Gloria and Eddie, his new basketball squeezed tightly between his hands.

"Eddie! Mama! Watch me duck!" LeBron squealed.

Eddie turned away and looked down at LeBron. "C'mon, Bron. Let's see what you got!"

LeBron suddenly pulled away from Eddie and ran straight to the basket in the living room. He jumped and slammed the little basketball through the hoop. He then turned around and flashed a broad smile at Eddie.

"Ducked on you!" he giggled.

Eddie just laughed.

Gloria walked through the kitchen and left the house out the back door. The December air was cold. She hugged herself, and looked up at the sky.

I promise I'll take care of Bron, Mama. He's my baby. I'll raise him right. You'll see, she thought.

The cold was stinging her face, and she could hear LeBron laughing and screaming inside. She went back into the house, the weight of the world heavy on her, wondering what the future would hold.

Wandering

"Hey, LeBron. You here for what I think you're here for?" the shopkeeper asked from behind the counter as eight-year-old LeBron entered the tiny corner store crowded with a mish-mash of goods.

LeBron smiled broadly. He walked over to a colorful section of shelved goods and drew out a box of his favorite cereal. He looked at the front of the box. There was Fred Flintstone and Barney Rubble, right where they belonged.

LeBron loved Fruity Pebbles. He especially loved them because there was usually something free inside the box.

Actually, if LeBron had his choice, he would be going to Swenson's every day instead of to this dingy store for food and snacks. He would have a cheeseburger and wash it down with a chocolate malt. But the closest Swenson's was way up off Route 8, so it was too far to walk alone from the one-bedroom Elizabeth Park apartment where his mother and he were currently staying. Besides, Swenson's didn't take food stamps, so that was kind of a problem. This store would have to do for now.

LeBron walked over to the clerk, put the box down on the counter, and dug into his pocket for the food stamps his mother had left him to buy his cereal and snacks with. He was conducting the transaction with the quiet confidence of an old pro.

While the clerk waited for LeBron to fish the food stamps from his pocket he asked, "Ain't you supposed to be in school?"

LeBron sighed. The clerk always asked him the same question and he always gave him the same answer.

"I'm home schooled," LeBron answered seriously.

"Uh, huh…" the clerk said dubiously.

LeBron knew that the clerk knew he wasn't

home schooled, but they had to go through this routine for the day to be set right, so he did it. LeBron was supposed to be in school but he didn't feel like going today. He'd been to so many different schools he figured that nobody would really miss him if he didn't show up.

He quietly put the food stamps on the counter. The clerk completed the cereal transaction. LeBron grabbed the Pebbles and started to head out of the store.

"You stay out of trouble now," the clerk told LeBron as he was leaving.

"I will," LeBron answered without looking back.

And LeBron meant it. There was trouble in all of the Akron neighborhoods he had lived in and he wanted no part of that. Gloria would always try to reassure him by saying, "You and me, Bron Bron. We're a team. You can't never break up a winning team like us."

Later that afternoon, when Gloria came back to the tiny apartment, she saw LeBron on the couch, playing video games.

"Hey, Bron, how was school today?"

LeBron kept his eyes firmly on the television screen. He knew if he looked at his mother she would know the truth. Maybe she did anyway.

"Good," he said as he jerked the video controller violently.

Then LeBron paused and looked at his mother.

"Mama, are we homeless?" he asked.

Gloria was taken aback. Since she and her brothers had lost the Hickory Street house when LeBron was four, she and Bron had been moving from place to place, but they weren't exactly living on the street. They could always stay with family, friends, friends of family, or friends of friends for a while. They mostly stayed in places in Elizabeth Park where she knew people could put her and LeBron up. Elizabeth Park wasn't exactly Merriman Heights, where the fine, upstanding citizens of Akron lived in large old mansions with indoor pools, but she and LeBron weren't sleeping in an alley, either.

When Grandma Freda died, Gloria was just 19.

Her older brother, Willie, was 22 and her baby brother, Curt, was only 12.

They had really tried to keep the house, but Freda's castle on the dirt road by the railroad tracks in Akron had become a nightmare of bad plumbing, a leaking roof, and crumbling walls.

During the winter a neighbor and family friend, Wanda Reaves, came to see how Gloria and LeBron were doing. What she saw appalled her. The house was a mess: dishes were piled high everywhere and there was a *hole* in the living room floor. And it was *cold,* because Gloria and her brothers couldn't afford to pay to heat the house.

"You have to get out of here," she told Gloria. "This place isn't safe for you and it certainly isn't safe for your baby. Go on. Pack. You're coming to live with me."

Gloria had actually been grateful for the no-nonsense order. She packed, gathered up little LeBron, and moved out to go live with Wanda that day. Gloria and LeBron never went back to the family home. Eventually, the Hickory Street house became so run down and dangerous that the city condemned it and bulldozed it to the ground. There was no returning to the only real home either of them had known.

Since then, Gloria was never quite sure where the two of them would end up or for how long. Sometimes she had a job and sometimes she didn't. But she always found a place for them to stay. LeBron had gotten so used to moving at the drop of a hat that he didn't even complain about it anymore. He had learned to simply gather his things and move on to the next place without asking any questions. Right now, they were staying in the apartment of yet another of Gloria's friends and LeBron was sleeping on the couch at night; or at least he was trying to sleep between the harsh background noise of the neighborhood streets and the loud parties in the other apartments.

Gloria was between jobs now and the two of them were getting by on welfare, food stamps, and the kindness of friends and family. She didn't want to tell LeBron that they didn't have much time left to stay at this apartment either and that they would have to move on again soon.

But, homeless? LeBron's question disturbed her. That wasn't what she wanted for her baby.

"No, baby. We're not homeless. Now where did you get that notion?" she answered.

LeBron shrugged. "Just thinking. We never stay one place too long."

"That's true, honey, but we have lots of people in our lives and they are always looking after us. So, we're not homeless, we just have one big, spread out family."

LeBron shrugged. "Okay, Mama."

A week later, Gloria quietly nudged LeBron awake as he slept on the couch.

"Get your stuff Bron Bron. It's time to go."

LeBron knew the drill. He rubbed his eyes, yawned, and started to gather his things and said to himself what he always said, "It's time to roll."

Who Likes Football?

Gloria sat on the steps of the building, watching
LeBron play tag with some of the other kids from
the surrounding apartments. It was hot and sticky
out, but that was typical for August in Akron.

She and LeBron were staying in the two-bedroom
apartment of a friend in a two-story downtown
Akron housing project. Gloria was worried, but
she wouldn't let LeBron on to that. It had been the
fifth move for her and LeBron in about five months.
Maybe more, she couldn't remember. And it
looked like they were about to be kicked out of this
apartment soon.

She let the thought go and started yelling
encouragement to the kids who were playing tag.
"C'mon, Bron Bron, you catch that boy and you

tag him good!" she called out. She laughed when LeBron turned around and gave her an exasperated look.

That boy is getting big, she thought. She was 5'5" and LeBron was only nine and just as tall as her. He towered over the other boys his age.

Gloria wasn't the only person watching the kids playing tag. Bruce Kelker was an assistant coach for an Akron pee wee football team called the East Dragons. He was leaning on his car watching a tall lanky kid move among the other kids. The kid was quick and he seemed to have a natural instinct for avoiding the other kids who were trying to tag him.

Bruce had been driving around the city looking for players under 10 years old who might be able to play on the team. He knew that Akron was full of talented inner-city kids who might not know that pee wee football leagues even existed. He was looking for diamonds in the rough; as he watched the tall kid move, he thought he might have discovered the gem he was looking for.

He watched a bit longer from his car, then

decided that he would go over and talk to the kids to see if any of them might be interested in joining his team. Well, he was really looking to see if the tall kid might be interested in joining his team at the very least.

He walked past Gloria and acknowledged her with a nod and a smile as he made a beeline toward the playing children in the common yard. They were yelling and running around like a herd of cats, each one darting in a different direction trying to avoid being tagged and becoming the dreaded "it."

"Hey, ya'll!" Bruce yelled trying to get the children's attention. "Hey! I need to talk to you!" The kids kept running and screaming, oblivious to the stranger who was trying to get their attention.

Bruce then stuck two fingers in his mouth and blew as hard as he could. The piercing whistle that came from his mouth stopped the kids dead in their tracks. They looked at Bruce much the same way Gloria had. Strangers usually meant trouble in this part of town.

"Awright!" Bruce said cheerfully. He clapped his hands together and exclaimed, "Who likes football?"

About six skinny arms shot up immediately.

The tall kid exclaimed, "That's my favorite sport!"

"How old are you, son?" Bruce asked him.

"I'm nine," he answered.

"Nine?!" Bruce exclaimed.

"Yes, sir," the kid said quietly.

Bruce thought the lanky kid was at least 11. He had been worried he might be too old to play on his team. But now...

This must be my lucky day, thought Bruce. *This has got to be fate.*

Bruce smiled broadly at the kid. "That's good. Because I coach for a football team called the East Dragons. Whose gonna be my Emmit Smith?"

What Bruce didn't know was that LeBron loved the Dallas Cowboys. He would spend hours sketching their logo in a little pad. But he actually wanted to be Eric Metcalf or Deion Sanders more than Emmitt Smith.

"Okay," Bruce said. "Tell you what. I'm going to line you all up and you guys are going to race across the parking lot. The first one to cross the finish line gets to be my running back!"

Bruce figured the parking lot was close to 100-yards long, give or take. He lined up the fidgeting boys who were itching to race. He ran to the other end of the parking lot, put his hand up and then brought it down sharply.

It wasn't even close. LeBron won the race by 15 yards. Bruce whistled softly, "*Have to have that kid,*" and gestured for the panting and sweating kids to gather around him.

Bruce looked at the tall kid and asked, "What's your name, son?"

"LeBron James," he managed to reply between gulps of air.

"Would you like to play some football for me, LeBron?" Bruce asked.

"Sure!" LeBron said. He thought his face was going to break he was smiling so hard.

Gloria, on the other hand, was not so sure about

the whole football idea. As usual, she did not mince words about her thoughts on the matter after Bruce approached her about letting LeBron play for his team.

LeBron was standing next to his mother as Bruce and she discussed the situation. Well, at least while *she* discussed the situation.

"The boy has never played a game of football in his life. What if he gets hurt?" she said, her hands defiantly on her hips.

Bruce opened his mouth, but Gloria interrupted.

"And besides, we can't afford it and I don't have a car. How is he gonna get to practice?"

Bruce opened his mouth again, but Gloria jumped in before he could utter a word.

"And another thing, you come waltzing in off the street and I don't know you from Adam and suddenly you're talking about whisking my Bron Bron off to play for some football team I've never heard of?"

"Mama!" LeBron interrupted.

The interruption took Gloria by surprise. Usually,

LeBron was shy and quiet and wouldn't ever interrupt a conversation between two adults.

Bruce took LeBron's interruption and Gloria's stunned silence as his cue to state his case.

"Look, Ms. James, don't worry about anything. I'll pick him up for practice and bring him back home. I'll store his equipment in my car. As far as the money goes, we can work something out."

The expression on her face told Bruce that she was not convinced. He leaned in and said earnestly, "I think LeBron has the possibility to be really good. You learn more valuable lessons playing football than what you learn on the streets. Believe me, I know. Who knows where it might lead?"

Gloria said nothing.

LeBron knew that was a good sign. When his mama said nothing it meant that she was seriously considering what to do and it wasn't a "No" yet.

"What you think, Bron Bron?" she said suddenly, turning toward him.

LeBron thought his heart was going to leap out of his chest.

"I wanna play football, Mama! Please! Pleeeaaaase!" he cried.

Gloria looked hard at LeBron. She could see the excited expectation on LeBron's face. It was a look she wished she would see more often.

The skeptical look on her face softened. She smiled and hugged LeBron, then turned to face Bruce, suddenly all business and serious once again.

"Okay, let's talk about when that first practice is and when you're going to pick him up."

For the second time that day, LeBron thought his smile was going to break his face.

Belonging

Coach Kelker was as good as his word.

At 3:45 on Monday he picked LeBron up to take him to practice. Gloria walked LeBron to Bruce's car and opened the passenger side door. LeBron slipped quietly into the back seat, looking sheepish. Then Gloria slipped into the front seat.

"Ummm…" Bruce said. "You coming, too?"

Gloria looked straight ahead. "Seriously? Did you really think I was going to put my boy in your car and just let you drive away with him?"

Bruce sighed. "But you can trust me. I promise."

"We'll see," Gloria answered.

Bruce shrugged and started the car. When it came to Gloria, he had the feeling that he would have to learn to pick his battles and not letting her come to LeBron's first practice was a battle he was sure to lose.

"Okay, let's go," he said.

Bruce looked into the rearview mirror and saw LeBron quietly looking out of the car window with a serious look on his face.

"How you feeling, young man?"

"Never played real football before," LeBron answered.

"You'll do fine. I guarantee it," Bruce said confidently.

But he was a little nervous, too. A lot of kids didn't have the work ethic, the attitude, or the support system at home to rise to the top.

He was hoping this kid, LeBron James, would be different.

After a 15-minute drive, Bruce, Gloria, and LeBron arrived at the practice field. Bruce parked the car and Gloria got out immediately, but LeBron hung back in the backseat of the car. He was watching the other kids on the field in their uniforms, milling about with their helmets off.

He was wondering how he would do or if he would get along with the other kids. He decided that he would keep a low profile, like he did at every new school he went to. Kids who didn't draw attention to themselves got through.

LeBron's train of thought was broken by a rap on the back passenger window.

"C'mon, LeBron, you coming?" Bruce said, his arms open.

LeBron took a deep breath, held it, and then exhaled slowly. He opened the back door and got out of the car.

LeBron was much taller than most of the other kids and when Coach Bruce told the team to take a lap around the field to warm up, LeBron finished way ahead of the pack. Gloria raised her hands in the air as if LeBron had just scored a touchdown. LeBron looked over at Gloria and shut his eyes hard. It could be a little difficult to blend in with his mother around.

Frank Walker, Sr. was standing next to Bruce

as they watched LeBron tear up the field on that initial lap. Frank worked with the Akron Housing Authority, but spent his spare time as an assistant coach for the East Dragons. "Where'd you find that kid?" Frank Sr. asked Bruce.

"Over in a project downtown. Name's LeBron James," Bruce answered.

"Can he play?"

"Don't know. Says he's never played football before."

"Well, he certainly looks like he can play," said Frank Sr. as he watched LeBron fly ahead of his other teammates. His son, Frankie Jr., who was also on the team, was expecting to start as tailback for the East Dragons this year. After watching LeBron, Frank Sr. knew that Frankie Jr. was going to be disappointed. The new kid was phenomenal.

Frank Sr. looked over at Gloria, who was fist pumping, cheering on her son.

"What's her story?" Frank said pointing in Gloria's direction.

Bruce whistled. "That's LeBron's mother, Gloria.

Believe me, you do not want to argue with that woman when it comes to her son."

"Like getting between a mother bear and her cub, huh?" Frank said, laughing.

"You have no idea," replied Bruce, shaking his head.

As the practice wore on, LeBron felt he had found his place. He knew he belonged here and it felt good.

The head coach, Willie Johnson, blew his whistle. "Okay, everybody gather round. Take a knee," he yelled.

The kids formed a semicircle around the coaches, helmets off, sweat beading on their foreheads.

"That was a good first practice. I think we have a good group here. Okay, everybody up, put your hands together, and let's yell, 'Dragons!' so that everybody can hear us."

The kids got up enthusiastically and cheered loudly.

Slowly, the players filtered away, leaving to go home with their parents. Bruce looked around for

LeBron and found him about 20 feet away with his mother, looking downcast.

He walked over to LeBron, leaned down and said, "What's the matter, LeBron? I thought you looked great out there today. Why are you looking so sad?"

LeBron looked at Coach Bruce and said quietly, "Just sad that practice is over. Can't wait for tomorrow. You're still going to come by and get me, right?"

Coach Bruce smiled and rubbed LeBron's head vigorously.

"Don't you worry, I'll be there every time to make sure you don't miss one practice. That's a promise."

LeBron smiled slightly and nodded.

"C'mon. Let's take you home," Bruce said.

The three of them walked to Coach Bruce's car. LeBron didn't say anything during the entire ride back.

Missing Star

Each day at 3:45, picking up Gloria with LeBron became part of Coach Bruce's routine. Gloria had signed up to be team mother and he had to admit that her enthusiasm for the job was infectious.

LeBron had turned out to be just as good as Coach Bruce thought he might be. The kid was motivated, smart, and wanted to learn everything he could about the sport. He had an intelligence about the game that was uncanny.

When they put him at tailback, he seemed to be able to predict which way the defenders were going and would cut to avoid them. He had a sense of where the holes were going to open up and would instinctively go there. He was big and fast and if he couldn't dodge a tackle, he would simply put his head down and run over a defender.

"Oh my, it's Eric Dickerson!" Coach Walker would yell.

He also had big hands for a kid his age and could catch a football as well as he could run with one. He proved to be a weapon in both the run game and the passing game.

In their first scrimmage against another team, LeBron broke free for an 80-yard touchdown run the very first time he was given the ball. The other side just watched in stunned silence as LeBron ran away from the pack, time and time again. If there had been any doubt whether LeBron was going to be a dominant force in the league, it had pretty much been put to rest then and there. The quiet, shy kid was a natural. There was no doubt about it.

It was another Monday, and Coach Bruce was on his way to pick up LeBron and Gloria for practice. He pulled into the parking lot of the project and was surprised that LeBron and Gloria weren't there yet. LeBron usually would be anxiously waiting for him to pull up, ready to jump into his car to get to practice.

But here it was, 3:45, and no LeBron or Gloria. He waited for about ten minutes and when they still hadn't come to meet him, he got out of the car and made his way to the apartment where they were staying. He knocked on the door and heard a rustling. Very slowly, the door opened up a crack and the woman behind the door looked at him for a moment and then recognized him.

She opened up the door wider and said, "If you're looking for Gloria and LeBron, they ain't here no more. Moved out this past weekend."

Coach Bruce stood at the door stunned. He knew that Gloria and LeBron's living arrangements weren't stable, but he had no idea that his star player would just be up and gone one day without any warning.

"Hold on," the woman at the door said. She

went inside and came back with a piece of paper, which she handed to him.

"Glo said to give you this when you came around looking for them. It's the address of where they're staying now."

Coach Bruce looked down at the piece of paper. Fortunately, their new place wasn't too far from where he was now. He thanked her and left.

He drove to the address written on the piece of paper and found another ramshackle building that had seen better days. He went to the listed apartment number and knocked on the door softly.

LeBron answered from the other side, "Who is it?"

"It's Coach Bruce, LeBron. Open up, please."

The door opened and a relieved looking LeBron faced him.

"You found us!" LeBron cried. "Mama said you would, but I was worried."

"Where is your mama?" Coach Bruce asked.

"She isn't here right now, but she told me to go along with you to practice when you found us."

He shook his head and said, "Okay, Bron. Let's go."

After they got into the car, Coach Bruce asked LeBron, "How many times have you moved this year?"

LeBron looked down at his lap and answered quietly, "Can't say. I think about three or four times. I don't really think much about it. I just go when Mama says it's time."

LeBron didn't offer anything more, so the two didn't talk about it the rest of the way to practice.

While the boys were doing warm-ups before practice, Coach Bruce pulled Frank Sr. aside.

"Almost didn't find LeBron today," he said to Frank. "Went to pick him up for practice and he and Gloria were gone from their place. Moved out. Lucky I found him."

Frank Sr. answered, "Really? Poor kid. That's rough."

"Maybe I can do something about it," Coach Bruce said.

When Coach Bruce walked LeBron to the door after practice and knocked, Gloria answered the door. He asked her if he could have a word with her alone.

"Just thinking of what might be best for LeBron right now." Coach Bruce said to her. "I think he's a great kid. You're obviously doing something right with that boy. He's very respectful and he listens. But it's good for kids to have structure. So, I thought it might be a good idea if he moved in with me for a while."

"You want to him to do WHAT?" Gloria asked in disbelief.

"Look. I'm just offering a place for LeBron to stay until you get a place of your own." Bruce said.

Gloria took the stance. Hands on hips. Making eye contact with those piercing eyes. She was digging in. Bruce knew that this was not going to be easy.

"No offense, Coach *Kelker*," Gloria practically spat, "but Bron Bron has been playing for you for, what, three or four weeks? I trust you as his coach, but living with you? Sorry, I don't know you well enough to just hand him over to you."

"I get that," Coach Bruce said, raising his hands in mock surrender. "I'm just offering to help. I have a two-bedroom apartment. He can have his own room and his own bed. It has to be better than sleeping on a different couch every other month, right?"

Coach Bruce hesitated, then added, "I talked to my girlfriend about it and…"

"Girlfriend?" Gloria exploded. "Uh, uh… nobody gonna replace me as Bron Bron's mama!"

Coach Bruce's shoulders slumped. He knew he was going to have to play a card that was sure to be very unpopular at home.

"Tell you what, Glo," he said slowly. "Why don't you both move in? You can share the bedroom. We have enough room."

Gloria looked startled, then immediately softened, relief replacing the look of aggravation on her face. "Really??"

Gloria looked directly at Coach Bruce and said,

"And what about your girlfriend? What is she going to say about another woman moving into your apartment?"

Coach Bruce said nothing for a long minute.

"Don't worry. I'll handle it," he finally said.

"I have my conditions too," Gloria said. "I will chip in some of my welfare payments for the rent."

He nodded.

"And I'll cook hamburgers twice a week."

"It's a deal!" Coach Bruce said with a smile. He looked at the beautiful, proud woman standing in front of him and felt he was doing the right thing.

Time to Roll... Again

LeBron loved football. Football was family.
Coach Bruce Kelker and Coach Walker were
like fathers to him. They listened to him and
they really cared about what happened to him.
Most of all, LeBron found out that he was really
good. He had scored 18 touchdowns for the East
Dragons during the season and they ended up 6-0.
It felt great when people recognized him for his
accomplishments.

LeBron found he liked that spotlight.

But he also found the spotlight could have its
bad side, too. LeBron had been so good that other
coaches in the league had openly questioned his age
and some had even demanded to see his
birth certificate.

Coach Bruce caught him once slumping down in the huddle and dipping his knees.

"What the hell are you doing?" Coach Bruce asked LeBron.

"Trying to blend in," LeBron said sheepishly.

"You ain't ever going to blend in," Bruce told him. "And that can be a good thing."

LeBron loved hearing the crowd cheer when he made a good run or a great catch. There was nothing better than watching the referee raise his hands in the air and having his teammates jump on him and fall on top of him after he scored a touchdown. He loved wearing the red and white colors of the East Dragons and especially loved the number 21 he got to wear—the same number that Deion Sanders wore.

He could hear his mama screaming on the sideline each time he made a break for the goal line. She would run with him step for step down the sideline, yelling at the top of her lungs, and then would jump up and down when he crossed into the end zone.

One time, she became so excited she smacked his shoulder pads so hard that he ended up flat on his back.

"Hey, wanna come over here? We can use you on defense!" the opposing coach had yelled from the far sideline. The whole crowd had laughed as she helped him up. It was a little embarrassing, but LeBron had learned to live with his mama's antics, because he knew that she was his biggest fan.

It had been an amazing season and LeBron felt as if something had started to *change* in him. But as time wore on, he also felt that things were changing in a way that had become very familiar to him. When they first moved into Coach Bruce's apartment, LeBron could sense that the coach's girlfriend was just being polite to him and his mama. He couldn't put his finger on it, but there was something going on between her and his mama that was never quite right. The longer they stayed with Coach Bruce, the more tense the situation got.

Sometimes, when LeBron was sitting alone in his room sketching Laker's logos, he could hear Coach Bruce and his girlfriend arguing in a hushed tone in the next room. He didn't know what the arguments were about, but he could guess.

It was late fall and the weather had been cool and was beginning to turn to the cold promise of winter in Akron.

So when football season was over, it was no surprise when Mama told LeBron that they would no longer be living with Coach Bruce. LeBron was in the bedroom packing up his meager belongings when there was a soft knock on the bedroom door and Coach Bruce entered the room.

He sat down on the bed next to LeBron. "Look, Bron. Sometimes, things don't work out between adults, but that has nothing to do with you."

LeBron nodded.

"You are special and always will be," he said as he put his arm around LeBron. "Just because you're moving out doesn't mean we won't be seeing each other. I'll be keeping in contact with you and your mama. And if you need anything, I'll be there. That's a promise."

LeBron promised himself he wouldn't cry. But it was all he could do to keep the dam in his eyes from bursting. He hugged Coach Bruce and went into the living room where Gloria was waiting.

Gloria looked at Coach Bruce quickly, nodded, and flashed a brief, sad smile.

The two of them left the apartment without saying a word.

It was time to roll. Again.

School's Out

LeBron and Frankie Jr., his assistant coach's son, had become good friends and LeBron would spend time hanging with his new friend over at the Walker's modest home. He was becoming an unofficial member of the Walker family.

When LeBron spent time at his house, Frank Sr. would see glimpses of the real kid hidden behind that shell of shyness. The real LeBron was funny and had an easy laugh. He was just an all-around good kid who kept out of trouble, was polite, and was eager to please.

Father and son were driving home together one night after dropping LeBron off at yet another borrowed place to live when Frankie Jr. suddenly ᴧed, "Daddy, how much school can you miss before you get in trouble?"

Frank Sr. thought that was an odd question. "Why you asking?"

Frankie fidgeted in the passenger seat. "Well," he said haltingly, "When I asked LeBron how he liked school and all, he told me that he really didn't know because he doesn't go to school much. Lots of days he stays put and plays video games all day."

"LeBron said that?" Frank asked.

Frankie nodded without looking at his father. "Is he going to get in trouble?"

"Naw," Frank said. "But you don't tell nobody else until I have time to think this over."

If the story was true, Frank thought, he would need to talk to Gloria. Gloria loved that boy and would give him all that she had. But right now, she didn't have much and she couldn't possibly provide him with the one thing that he really needed: a stable home.

LeBron had thrived playing for the East Dragons.

Some kids chafe against coaching and direction, but LeBron had been one of the most coachable kids he had ever encountered. He listened and learned and was always seeking to improve his skills. You just had to tell him how to do something once and he got it.

He had the feeling that, given the opportunity, LeBron would thrive. But first, he needed to find out if LeBron was missing as much school as Frankie Jr. had said he might be missing. He had an idea that might help LeBron and Gloria. First he would need to talk to his wife, Pam, and the rest of his family about what he thought needed to be done. He hoped it would all work out.

LeBron ran into Frankie Jr.'s bedroom, leaving Gloria alone with Frank Sr. in the kitchen of his home. Pam had just offered Gloria a cup of coffee and had left the two of them to sit down at the table. Pam knew what the discussion was going to be about, but since she barely knew Gloria, she thought it best that Glo and Frank have some time between themselves before she interjected herself into the conversation.

"I understand that LeBron has missed more of his fourth grade classes than he's been to," Frank said to Gloria. "He's missed 87 days of school to be exact."

She nodded but didn't look surprised.

"Can I ask you a question, Glo?"

"Please do."

"How many times have you moved this year?"

She thought for a moment. "Half a dozen, I guess," she said.

He felt a knot in his throat. "Where is his father?"

She told him that LeBron didn't know who his real father was and she wasn't ready to talk about it. And the man he called his dad wasn't available most of the time. Right now he was in jail.

Frank cleared his throat and spoke slowly. "I know things have been hard for you and LeBron. I know that you're trying to find a permanent place where you both can live. But right now this situation isn't working out. For either of you. I think you know that."

Frank noticed tears welling in Gloria's eyes. "The boy needs some stability," Frank said.

"I know," Gloria interjected softly.

"I want to give him a safe place to stay and a family to help him feel secure," Frankie Sr. continued. "I've talked to Pam about it and we would love to have LeBron stay with us. He and Frankie Jr. get along great and they would be just like brothers. I think that Frankie Jr. would like that, seeing as he has two sisters who gang up on him. We can set up an extra bed in Frankie's room."

Gloria opened her mouth to speak, but Frank raised his hand quickly and said, "You can visit Bron any time you like. This arrangement is temporary and if you decide you don't like it, it ends when you decide it ends. Period."

Gloria swallowed hard and looked down at her hands, which were resting on the kitchen table. "Do you think I'm a bad mama?"

"Naw, Glo. We all need help sometimes. No

judgment. We think LeBron is a great kid and you've obviously given him good values. But he needs more. He needs routine."

Gloria looked up at the ceiling and sighed heavily. "Five days a week without my baby? He's the only thing I've got," she hesitated, her words catching in her throat. "But… I think you're right, Frankie. LeBron hasn't had a real home since Mama died and we lost the house. He thinks the way we live is normal. We both know it isn't."

Her eyes met Frank's. "Yes," she said resolutely.

"Yes?" Frank replied quizzically.

Gloria nodded. "Yes. LeBron can live with you. You're right. It's for the best. You'll make sure he gets to school like he's supposed to?"

Frank nodded.

"And he'll be able to keep playing football for you and the East Dragons?" Gloria asked.

Frank shook his head. "No."

"But Bron Bron loves playing football! Why can't he play for the East Dragons anymore if he stays with you?" Gloria protested.

Frank smiled widely. "Because I'm taking over as coach of the South Rangers. He and Frankie will be Rangers, just like when I was a kid."

Frank suddenly got very serious. He looked directly at Gloria. "We're going need a team mom. You have any suggestions?"

Gloria laughed. "Maybe a couple."

Frank laughed. "Let me get Pam and we can talk about this all together."

Frank stood up to go get his wife, but Gloria had leapt out of her chair and was hugging Frank before he had made two steps towards the living room.

"Thank you, Frankie," she whispered as she squeezed him hard.

"Let's ask the boy," Frank said.

Family Life

It was 6:30 in the morning and the early sun was still low on the horizon. Pam came into Frankie Jr's room, turned on the light, and said in a no-nonsense tone, "Time to get up!"

Frankie Jr. knew that there was no use arguing with his mother. He rolled out of bed, rubbed his eyes, and went over to the other bed that was occupying his room. Underneath the covers, LeBron was still asleep and not moving.

"Bron," Frankie said as he shook LeBron. "Time to get up. C'mon. We gotta get ready to go to school."

LeBron rustled, opened one eye, and then mumbled, "It's still nighttime."

Frankie Jr. yawned. "Not playing, Bron. We have to get up. You know that."

Frankie reached down and shook LeBron.

"When I moved in with you, nobody told me I was living on a farm. Do I have to milk the cows now?" LeBron chuckled tiredly.

Frankie Jr. just rolled his eyes. "Seriously, Bron. You know the drill. If my mama has to come back to get you up she is not going to be happy."

LeBron stirred and then sat up slowly. It was going to be his first day of fifth grade at Portage Path Elementary and he really didn't want to be late. Somehow, he had passed the fourth grade even after missing 87 days of school. This was a new school year, a new school, and a new grade. When he moved in with the Walkers they told him that things were going to be different.

And they had been.

The move itself hadn't been hard for LeBron. He was used to moving from place to place and the Walker's house was just one more place to move to. Sure, he missed his mama during the weekdays, but he still got to be with her during the weekends and sometimes more.

What LeBron wasn't used to was that he suddenly had a *schedule* he was expected to keep. Pam and Frank Walker expected him to do chores right along with Frankie Jr. and his sisters, Chanelle and Tanesha. There was a time to do homework and a time to go to bed, and no amount of complaints or arguments altered that. If you didn't wash up the night before, Mrs. Walker would get you up at 6:00 in the morning instead of 6:30 so you could take care of business before the day got started.

Late at night when the kids were in bed, Pam Walker told Frankie Sr. that she was in awe at how quickly LeBron had adjusted to life with them.

"What made it easy is that he loves the chores," she said. "He really didn't fight me at all." She smiled, "I need to tell Frankie Jr. to clean up the room. LeBron keeps his side neat. Always."

"He is a great kid," Frankie Sr. agreed.

What surprised LeBron was that he found he loved having a schedule and responsibilities.

He was part of a family now and it felt great.

He Got No Game

LeBron was frustrated, but he wasn't going to give up.

Frankie Jr. faked going right, then suddenly darted left.

LeBron had gone for the fake and could only watch helplessly as Frankie dribbled the ball past him and drove to the basket for another two.

"14-4," Frankie yelled out.

LeBron wanted to cry. He hated losing and yet here he was getting whipped on the basketball court by his best friend who was way smaller than him. When LeBron had the ball, he could barely dribble. He was fast, but uncoordinated. When Frankie Jr. defended him it was like his brain and his body were somehow disconnected. He knew what he wanted to do, but his body wasn't getting the message.

Frankie missed his next shot and LeBron got the rebound. He dribbled the ball and tried to make a quick move to the basket, but Frankie was able to steal the ball easily, go to the hoop, and bank in another two.

"16-4," Frankie called out.

What was going on? Michael Jordan, his favorite player, made it look so easy. LeBron was starting to realize that making it look easy wasn't as easy as it looked.

He thought that Frankie Jr. was enjoying this a little too much. Every time he would make an easy two, he would smile a little; not so much that he was outright dissing him, but just enough to let LeBron know that there was nothing he could do to stop him.

Frank Sr. watched the one-on-one game in silence as it progressed. He was assessing LeBron's basketball skills as he and Frankie Jr. battled on

the playground court. Besides being a pee wee
football coach, Frank Sr. also coached the
Summit Lake Hornets, a youth recreational league
basketball team.

He knew this one-on-one game was unfair from
the outset. He had been coaching little Frankie
for years on the finer points of the game. Frankie
was years ahead of the curve when it came to his
basketball skills. LeBron was clearly outclassed.

He was obviously full of raw athletic talent, but
it was also equally as obvious that he had never
been taught any fundamental basketball skills.
Nevertheless Frank Sr. was confident that if LeBron
took to basketball the way he took to football, he
would learn the skills he would need to be a good
player in no time.

But, right now, the boy had no game and Frankie
Jr. was schooling him.

He could see that LeBron was getting more
and more frustrated as the game continued.
LeBron didn't much like losing. Beneath that
quiet exterior and seemingly laid-back demeanor,

there was a keen competitor. Even at the age of nine, there was an intensity in LeBron's eyes beyond his years.

Frank Sr. noticed that LeBron didn't give up. Other kids may have left the court crying or may have started taking out their frustrations in hard fouls against an opponent. But LeBron was watching and learning. He would study a move Frankie put on him and then would adjust to stop Frankie if he tried it again. While Frankie was still scoring on LeBron, the baskets were coming a little bit harder as the game progressed. Even in this short time, LeBron was learning to anticipate; to sense where he was on the court; to step in to cut off easy angles to the hoop.

Frankie Jr. drove hard to the basket and LeBron tried to keep up with him. Suddenly, Frankie stopped. LeBron tried to stop with him, but lost his balance and fell backwards on to his rear end. Frankie hefted an uncontested 10-foot shot and it went in, all net.

"Game!" Frankie shouted, "24-6!"

LeBron didn't even attempt to get up from his sitting position. He hugged his knees and lowered his head.

Frank Sr. went over to him, squatted down, and put both of his hands on LeBron's shoulders.

"Look at me, Bron. You know what you did wrong on that last play?"

LeBron looked directly at Frank Sr. and shook his head back and forth slowly.

"You were defending Frankie standing straight up. You have to keep your knees bent and your weight on the balls of your feet. If your weight is on your heels you are already falling backwards. As soon as Frankie stops you have nowhere to go but down."

Frank Sr. motioned for LeBron to stand up and for Frankie Jr. to come closer.

"Okay, Frankie, you're on offense. LeBron, you're on defense. Here's the defensive position you need to be in to try to stop him." Frank Sr. mimicked the defensive position then physically manipulated LeBron into the posture he wanted him in.

"Hands up! Legs apart! Toes forward! Off your heels! Shuffle! Don't cross your feet! Disrupt the dribble. Knees bent! Look at his waist, not his head!" Coach Walker yelled commands as LeBron worked hard to execute them. They worked on his defense until the muscles in LeBron's legs were burning and he was gasping for air. LeBron didn't much like defense. Offense was a lot more fun.

Defending Frankie was still hard, but as time wore on, LeBron could feel something change. He was starting to see what Frankie was going to do. He realized that it could work the other way, too. If you were on offense, you should be able to anticipate what a defender would do and then you could beat him.

"Okay, let's go home," Frank Sr. bellowed. "Next time we'll work more on offense and some dribbling drills."

He hesitated and then looked directly at LeBron.

"And we have to start working on your left hand, Bron. You can't be great until you can make a layup with your weak hand."

"What?" LeBron cried. "I'm still not so great with my right hand!"

"You need to work on both hands. A basketball player who can only shoot with one hand is only half a ball player," Frank said as he slapped LeBron on the back.

Frankie Jr. pointed at LeBron and went, "Aaaaaaaaaa."

LeBron shot Frankie a dirty look and then rolled his eyes.

That's stupid, he thought. *When will I ever have to use my left hand to make a layup?*

The Team

LeBron and Frankie Jr. were rushing out of the house to play basketball in the driveway of the Walker home, but were met by a brick wall named Pam Walker. "You two *have* done all of your homework, right?" she said, arms crossed.

Frankie Jr. looked sheepish, then looked down at his feet. "I, uh, well…"

"That's what I thought," Pam said sternly. "And what about you, LeBron?"

"Finished," he beamed.

"All right, then. You. Frankie. Back up to your room until your homework is done."

Frankie turned around slowly, looking dejected as he started to head back up the stairs to his bedroom.

"And I want to see it when it's done!" Pam called after him.

"And you," she said looking at LeBron, "I want you to show me yours. Now."

LeBron didn't say a word, turned on his heels, and ran upstairs. He came back with two workbooks and several papers.

Pam looked over the work briefly and liked what she saw.

LeBron tore out of the front door as fast as he could, basketball in hand.

She had to smile. LeBron had gone from a boy who never wanted to go to school to a solid B student at Portage Elementary. He hadn't missed a day of school and he actually *liked* going to school now. He had told her that he especially liked the music and art classes Portage offered.

Pam looked out of the kitchen window and watched the lone figure playing basketball in the cold afternoon air. LeBron was practicing driving to the basket and putting layups into the hoop. She was fascinated by the boy's discipline. He would make the layup, grab the ball, pause as if he were thinking of something and then dribble back to begin driving to the basket again, trying a different approach.

It had only been a few months since Frank Sr. had taken LeBron and Frankie Jr. out to the playground for that first frustrating one-on-one match, but LeBron was now clearly the best player on the Hornets. Oh sure, he had complained mightily when Frank insisted that he learn how to shoot a left-hand layup and there had been some tears during defensive drills, but he had listened and learned.

Frank Sr. shook his head as LeBron stole the ball at half-court, drove to the basket, and scored on a *left-handed* layup.

He had coached a lot of kids at Summit Lake, but he had never coached one who learned everything so quickly. You just had to show LeBron how to do something once and he got it. He had a game I.Q. that was off the charts. Frank Sr. had even made

LeBron a coach to help with a team of eight year olds. He was only nine, but the kids already looked up to him.

"Never seen anything like that boy," he said to Pam one day when they were sitting together at the kitchen table. "He's going places. Most natural athlete I've ever coached. Football. Basketball. Doesn't matter."

Of course, Frank would never tell LeBron any of those things. The one thing Frank believed in was T-E-A-M. He had seen what happened to athletes who got full of themselves and he was not going to let that happen to LeBron. He watched as LeBron gathered a rebound on the other end and dribbled down the court. He passed off to a teammate who passed back off to him as he drove to the basket. LeBron could have easily scored on the layup, but went up, drawing two defensive players to the key to stop him, then dished the ball off to another teammate who was wide open on the low post.

The teammate made the easy bucket.

Frank Sr. shot up from his seat and yelled, "That's what I'm talking about! Nice pass!"

But this was rare. If LeBron had any weakness as a player it was that he could be a ball hog. Who doesn't like to score? But the other kids on the team were getting frustrated when LeBron would shoot the ball almost every time it was fed to him.

After yet another game where LeBron took shot after shot without looking for open teammates, Frank pulled him aside for a one-on-one talk.

"Look, Bron," Frank explained. "You remember how I said a player who only knew how to shoot with one hand was only half a player?"

LeBron nodded, and Frank continued, "Same goes for a player who doesn't help his teammates get better. If you shoot every time you get the ball, no matter how good you are, you are hurting the team. See what I'm saying?"

"Not really, Coach," LeBron answered quietly. "If I'm scoring, then we can win."

Frank sighed and put a hand on LeBron's shoulder. "The difference between a winner and a loser is that a winner doesn't forget that he is part of something bigger and doesn't try to do it all.

LeBron said nothing, but nodded slowly.

The next time the Hornets played, Frank saw a change in the way LeBron approached the game. He was still making hot dog moves and taking some ill-advised shots, but now he was also drawing defenders to himself, finding an open teammate, and then dishing the ball to them for easy baskets.

The Summit Lake Hornets were winning another game. So far they were undefeated and were looking at a pretty clear shot at winning the rec league championship.

Frank Sr. was sitting on a foldout chair, shouting out instructions to his players from the side.

"You need to block your man out if you want to get that rebound," he shouted to LeBron.

LeBron looked over at the bench and nodded. Frank Sr. was positive that next time, LeBron's man would be blocked out.

The final buzzer went off and the Hornets had

won by 14 points. They were laughing and high-fiving as they approached the bench.

LeBron shouted, "That was fun!"

"Didn't I say so?" Frank said as he high-fived LeBron.

LeBron and Frank looked at each other; a brief understanding smile passed between them.

"C'mon, team, put your hands in the circle. Let them know who you are!" Frank yelled.

"Hornets!" they screamed loudly.

Frank turned to Frankie Jr. and LeBron. "Hey, you wanna go to Swensen's to celebrate?"

He didn't have to ask twice.

The Coach

Dru Joyce II watched as LeBron made an easy layup to score two.

It was clear from the start of the game that LeBron was the best player on both sides of the court, but he was still a work in progress. He was tall and he was quick and coordinated, which was not always a combination that kids his age possessed. He wasn't afraid to go to the basket, even when going to the basket sometimes meant leaving wide-open teammates on the floor with their arms and mouths open, staring in disbelief that he hadn't passed off to them.

But the Summit Lake Hornets were simply dominating this game and much of that had to do with the tall, lanky kid with the big ears.

Dru Joyce was looking for players. He had just inherited the head coaching job of the Under-11 Northeast Ohio Shooting Stars travel basketball team. He and his son, Little Dru, were in the stands at the Summit Lake Recreation Center basketball court to see if LeBron might be a good addition to the team.

LeBron wasn't a complete stranger to either of them. He had impressed Dru when he had played against his son's team at the Ed Davis Recreational Center. Dru had heard through Akron's tight-knit youth sports grapevine that LeBron was kind of a legend on the football field. Fortunately, the AAU basketball season wouldn't interfere with football season. Coach Dru understood that LeBron's Summit Lake basketball coach, Frank Walker, was also his football coach and Coach Walker would never want to give up his star football player to basketball.

He had to admit he was just a little envious. LeBron was good at basketball *and* football. Football had been his sport, but Little Dru showed no interest in it at all.

"What do you think, Dru?" Coach Dru asked his son.

Little Dru stared down at the court with his usual serious expression. "He's got game," he replied curtly.

"But?" Coach Dru inquired, because there was always a "but" with Little Dru.

"But he's a ball hog," Little Dru answered.

Coach Dru smiled. If LeBron and Little Dru ended up being teammates, he was sure that Little Dru would have no problem telling him what he thought about ball hogs. He hadn't been nicknamed "The General" for nothing.

What Coach Dru liked about LeBron was that he was *thinking* about the game and adjusting. Sizing things up. Looking for open lanes. Looking to pass to the open man. Sometimes. More importantly, when Coach Walker yelled out an instruction to LeBron on the court, he actually *listened* and then *acted* on those instructions. The kid was *coachable* and that was a gift—especially for a new coach who wasn't quite sure of his footing.

There was a look of determination on LeBron's face as he dribbled down the court or went up for a rebound. Coach Dru could tell, just by watching how he carried himself on the court, that LeBron had the exact same attitude as his son, Little Dru: It was only fun when you won.

He had a feeling that the two of them might really click together on the court. They would push each other to become better players.

When the final buzzer sounded, the Summit Lake Hornets had won the game easily. Coach Dru had lost count of how many points LeBron had scored, but that didn't matter. He knew well before the end of the game that LeBron needed to be a Shooting Star.

He made his way down to the Hornet's bench to talk to Frank Walker and LeBron about joining his team. He had a very good feeling about the kid. He hoped that feeling would be mutual.

The Three Musketeers

LeBron had been excited when Coach Dru told him about the Shooting Stars and how he would get to travel to exotic locations like *Cleveland* to play games against other teams. He had never set foot out of Akron, and in his mind, Cleveland was like a mythical city from a fairy tale.

Coach Walker had agreed with Coach Dru that playing on a travel basketball team would be a great opportunity for LeBron "as long as it didn't interfere with football season or school." He also told Coach Dru that even though LeBron was living with him for the time being, he would still have to get Gloria's permission before LeBron could join the Shooting Stars.

Gloria took a liking to Coach Dru and his calm

manner, but took her time to make a decision. When she eventually said yes, LeBron had the same swelling feeling in his heart that he had when she had said yes to his playing pee wee football.

When they arrived at the first Shooting Star practice at the Salvation Army gym on Maple Street in Akron, Gloria looked around, then looked at Coach Dru and said matter-of-factly, "Kind of a ragtag gym you got here."

Dru could only shrug in response.

He couldn't deny it. It *was* a ragtag gym in a rough part of town with a linoleum floor instead of a real wood one. It was so small that the court itself wasn't even regulation size; but it was the only gym he could get his hands on to hold practices for his team.

But to LeBron, the gym was a palace brimming with possibilities. It was going to lead to places like Cleveland! What wasn't to like? LeBron was determined to make a good impression at his first Shooting Star practice. He kept trying to make impossible shots and made sloppy behind-the-back passes to his teammates during their first scrimmage together. When he dribbled the ball down the court by himself again and put up another awkward and badly missed shot, he suddenly found himself confronted by Coach Dru's son who was playing point guard on his scrimmage team. The small, skinny kid with big ears was standing about six inches from him... and he didn't look happy.

"You done yet?" he said looking straight up at LeBron. He stood about as tall as LeBron's chest.

"Done with what?" LeBron answered.

Little Dru's eyes narrowed. "Are you done with the Michael Jordan stuff, so we can start playing for real instead of us all watching you hog the ball and tossing bricks up at the basket?"

LeBron didn't know what to say. "I, uh..."

"Good," Little Dru shot back. "Then let's play some basketball," He turned around and walked away without saying another word.

LeBron stood on the court with his mouth open.

The silence was broken by a loud laugh to LeBron's right. He turned to face the laughter

and saw that it was a big kid who was laughing
so hard. He was as big as Little Dru was small.
He was taller than LeBron and was hard to miss
at about six feet tall. And he looked almost as wide
as he was tall.

"What're you laughing at?" LeBron said, irritated.

"You!" the big kid laughed. "You should have
seen the look on your face!"

LeBron was about to shoot back with an angry
comment, but the big kid cut him off before he
could speak.

"Hey, don't get mad." he chuckled. "I always get
yelled at by Little Dru. Every time I drop a pass or
miss a layup he has something to say to me. And it
usually ain't nice."

The big kid stepped closer to LeBron. "I know
Little Dru from church. Can't figure out if he's
brave, stupid, or crazy. He just doesn't back down.
But he's all right. Mostly. In between the times you
don't feel like killing him."

LeBron had to admit that *he* wouldn't be crazy
enough to mess with the big kid standing beside

him. He had a feeling that Little Dru, on the other hand, would stand toe-to-toe with Godzilla if Godzilla dissed him.

"By the way," the big kid said. "My name's Sian Cotton."

"LeBron James," LeBron said as the two bumped fists. He had the feeling he was going to end up liking Sian.

The whistle blew and Coach Dru yelled, "Are you two going to talk all night or are we going to play some basketball?"

The scrimmage started up again and Little Dru dished a pass to Sian as he moved to the basket. Sian dropped the pass and the ball rolled harmlessly out of bounds at the baseline.

"You got no hands, Shamu!" Little Dru yelled.

"Couldn't see your pass coming at me from two feet off the ground! And who you calling Shamu, Smurf!" Sian yelled back.

"Who you calling Smurf?" Dru shot back, as he started walking toward Sian.

LeBron rolled his eyes and smiled.

LeBron found he had been right about Sian. He was funny and loud and once LeBron found out that Sian loved Swensen's cheeseburgers, he knew he had found a brother for life.

And Little Dru? Well, Little Dru demanded perfection from everybody around him, including himself. LeBron admired his mad skills and soon realized that the two of them had an unreal chemistry on the court. Mutual respect gradually turned into genuine friendship.

It was a strange brotherhood at first—Little Dru and Sian and LeBron. Little Dru was so quiet and intense and Sian was so big and loud. But somehow it just worked. LeBron, who had been quiet and cautious at first, found that he could open up and be himself around these guys.

They got so close that people started calling them the Three Musketeers.

"Muska what?" Sian had yelled the first time he heard that. "Why they calling us a candy bar?" Little Dru and LeBron could only shrug. They couldn't figure it out either.

What they all had in common was a sheer desire to win and improve. As they began to click on the court, the Shooting Stars started to win and get a reputation as the team to beat in the area.

The three of them soon found they were hanging out together off the court, too. It just felt like the natural thing to do. They would spend nights at Coach Dru's house, playing video games in the basement and goofing. Eventually, Coach Dru would come down and tell them it was time to go to sleep. But, mostly they stayed up all night, whispering and laughing.

LeBron had learned long ago that you never knew what life was going to dish out. Suddenly, he had gone from being an only child to having three new brothers in Frankie Jr., Sian, and Little Dru.

Life was good.

Matching Warm-ups
and Everything

"Whooeee! Who farted?" Sian yelled, as he made a face like he had just eaten a lemon dipped in salt.

Little Dru rolled his eyes and said nothing, while LeBron laughed hysterically.

"He who smelt it, dealt it!" LeBron yelled at Sian as he waved his hand back and forth in front of his face like he was swatting away invisible flies.

"Smells like cheese puffs dipped in smelly socks to me," Sian cried.

Little Dru just happened to have a bag of cheese puffs in his hands.

Sian burst out laughing. "That was so nasty I think I'm going blind!" he blinked his eyes hard and put his hands out in front of him, purposely hitting Little Dru in the back of his head. "My face is melting!"

Little Dru swiveled in his seat and swatted Sian's hands away. "In your case that would be an improvement."

"Ooooohhhh," LeBron said as he pointed to Sian and laughed even harder.

Sian suddenly looked hurt and said sweetly, "Now you gone and hurt my feelings, Little Dru. Didn't know leprechauns could be so mean!"

"Leprechaun? Who you calling leprechaun?" Little Dru threw the bag of cheese puffs at Sian and it hit him upside the head.

The whole team started laughing hysterically.

The only one in the minivan who was not laughing was Coach Dru.

"That's enough of that!" he said sternly. "No throwing stuff in the van. You're going to get us all killed before we get halfway to Florida!"

The van suddenly got quiet.

"Whoooeee," Sian yelled. "There goes another one!"

And the van fell out again.

LeBron was excited and scared at the same time. The Shooting Stars were going to Cocoa Beach, Florida, to play in the AAU Under-11 National Championship Tournament. Somehow, they had qualified, despite the fact they had not really played that many games together as a team since the sixth graders had branched off to form their own team. They were lucky to get enough kids to make a whole team. As it was, there were only seven kids on the Shooting Stars.

He was also excited because they were all going to Florida, which was way farther away than Cleveland. He had never stepped foot out of Ohio, and now they were going to the end of the United States. One thousand miles from home to be exact. And it was the first time in his life he was going to see the ocean! It was going to be fun playing against other AAU teams from across the nation. Coach Dru said that there were 64 teams competing.

That made LeBron a little nervous. Would the Shooting Stars be good enough to hold their own, or would they get blown out and laughed at for being some little team from Akron that had no right to be in the same gym with the big boys? He felt added pressure because he believed they had to show the world that Akron wasn't some kind of joke. The Shooting Stars had to represent.

He also was a little afraid to be so far from home. Sure, he was with his best friends, but he would still be far from the Walkers, far from his mama, and far from everything he was familiar and comfortable with. The smell and look and feel of Akron was in his blood. In LeBron's mind, Cocoa Beach might as well be on the moon.

The van got quiet inside as the hours wore on and they moved down I-77. Everybody was bored and tired and most of the team was sleeping as miles and miles became more miles and miles of tedious travel. LeBron looked out the van window sleepily, his head resting against the cool window as the sun crept down in the west and the sky darkened in degrees. He watched the sun go down and went to sleep to the music of tires on asphalt.

Leaning on the wheel, Coach Dru fought his fatigue. To think, they almost had not made this journey at all. He had been convinced that the Shooting Stars would have to pass on this opportunity. It was just too far away and would cost too much money.

Maybe next year, he had thought.

But a teammate's father had convinced him that the Shooting Stars should really go to the national tournament. Yes, the team couldn't afford to fly there, but they could drive. And yes, it would be a long and tedious journey. But what if this opportunity never came again? What if the Shooting Stars were just like their name—a flash in the night sky that burns briefly and brightly and then disappears forever?

Could Coach Dru live with asking the question, "What if?" for the rest of his life?

He had decided that he couldn't.

And now, here they were. In a minivan with miles to go, but heading toward a grand adventure that none of them would ever forget.

The opening ceremony for the tournament was held at the Kennedy Space Center and it was impressive. None of them had been to such a big deal in their entire lives. It was like being in the Olympics with 64 different teams marching in from all over the country.

LeBron was a bit overwhelmed.

He had to admit that some of those uniforms the other teams wore were awfully fine with tear-away warm-ups and matching basketball shoes. He couldn't help but make comparisons. Their shoes didn't match and were dirty and scruffy compared to the shiny, unscuffed shoes sported by the other teams. Their warm-ups were whatever they could find lying around the house; usually a hoodie with mismatched sweatpants.

LeBron thought the Shooting Stars were like Cinderella at the ball. Only they had showed up in a pumpkin disguised as a minivan and no fairy godmother had bothered to dress them up for the occasion. But uniforms don't make a team. LeBron was determined that the Shooting Stars were not going to embarrass themselves or Akron at this tournament.

"Yeah, they look all pretty, "LeBron whispered to Little Dru who looked envious. "But we can take them. No problem."

Soon, people were starting to talk about the little team from Akron that seemingly came out of nowhere and started winning games. It was like Little Dru and LeBron were connected by psychic powers. Little Dru could just sense when LeBron was going to break to the basket and then dish off a pass to him for an easy two. LeBron would drive to the basket and just know when Little Dru was wide open. Sian was even getting better as the tournament wore on, although he was most effective at being a large mountain blocking access to the basket.

They started moving up in the brackets. And everyone started paying attention. Who was this ragtag bunch of kids from Ohio who had come out of nowhere and were burning up the court? Who was this kid LeBron James?

They played like every game was their last and at the end of the tournament, the Shooting Stars had placed ninth among the 64 teams that competed for the AAU under-11 championship. Not bad for a team that had played only eight games together before the tournament.

At the end of the tournament, the Shooting Stars and Coach Dru were tired, but they were happy that they had done so unexpectedly well. Coach Dru was glad they had come to play, even if it now meant a 1,000-mile drive back to Akron. They all piled into the van for the journey back. The team was quiet as Coach Dru pulled out onto the highway to start home. He was praying that the team was so worn out that the quiet would last a while.

"Whooooeeeee!" Sian suddenly yelled. "Who cut the cheese?"

The van exploded into laughter.

Coach Dru sighed. It was going to be a long drive home.

A Place of Our Own

"What do you think, Bron Bron?" Gloria said beaming.

LeBron walked through the government-subsidized, two-bedroom apartment with his mother. It wasn't much to look at from the outside, with its big, blocky, concrete façade, but Spring Hill apartment #602 was going to be his new permanent address.

Gloria grabbed LeBron by the arm and rushed him into one of the empty bedrooms.

"This bedroom is yours. It's the bigger one!" Gloria exclaimed.

LeBron looked around. "Thanks, Mama."

LeBron followed his mother around the apartment as she showed him everything—

the bathroom, the kitchen, her bedroom, the closets, the silverware drawers.

"And look at this view!" she exclaimed as she pointed to a partial view of the city from the living room window.

LeBron smiled and nodded enthusiastically. His mama was so happy and excited that it was infectious. She was brimming with enthusiasm for the new life she and LeBron were going to share together.

LeBron was happy to finally be moving in permanently with his mama, but he also felt a lingering sadness and some doubt. Moving to Spring Hill meant that he would no longer be living with the Walkers. He had been living with them for 18 months and Pam and Frankie Walker were like second parents to him. Frankie Jr. was like the brother he never had.

The Walkers had welcomed LeBron into their home, but they had never let him forget that his last name was still James and that he had a mother who loved him. Gloria didn't let him forget either, picking him up to stay with her on the weekends whenever possible and making sure she attended as many of his games as she could.

Still, the Walkers had taken in a confused kid who had practically flunked out of fourth grade and had turned his life around. He had also learned something interesting about himself; if he buckled down and worked hard, he could get good grades in school. What really surprised him was that now he actually wanted to do well in school.

The Walkers had given him the gift of family and stability when he needed it the most and he would always be grateful. They would always be family.

He couldn't help it, but he had some lingering doubts about the move. Gloria had already tried to take him back to live with her permanently before this, but he had gone back to living with the Walkers when her living plans hadn't panned out. Was this move into the Spring Hill apartments going to be more of the same? While he was living with the Walkers, LeBron had found that he liked knowing where he was going to be day-to-day.

Gloria suddenly stopped buzzing around the apartment like a maniacal bee. She sensed that something was bothering LeBron and she had a pretty firm idea of what that might be.

She hugged him hard.

"Look, Bron. I promise this is for real. No more moving around," she said. "It's you and me and nothing's going to pull us apart again. We're here to stay. I promise."

Gloria had promised things before and sometimes those promises were kept and sometimes they weren't. LeBron knew his mama always meant well though. She really believed in those promises when she made them and was genuinely surprised and disappointed when she couldn't keep one.

LeBron leaned into her hug. "I know, Mama," he said softly. "You and me."

It was hard when it was time to leave the Walkers. Frank Sr. and Frankie Jr. and LeBron's uncles helped them move into their new place. They found beds and a sofa and a kitchen table at second-hand stores and some friends contributed things like dishes and silverware they would need to help them along in their new, independent life.

For the first time since he could remember, LeBron had his own bedroom. He walked into the room over and over again just to make sure that it was real and that it was his. His sports trophies were still on the floor, waiting for a shelf to put them on. He smiled as he looked at the wall above his bed. A poster of his favorite player, Michael Jordan, was pinned to the wall. Number 23 was flying, captured forever in midair, looking like he had been launched from a cannon, his arm high, and his hand firmly gripping the ball that was seemingly 10 feet above the basket. You could almost feel the thunderous dunk that was coming.

LeBron closed his eyes.

One day. One day I'll play with MJ.

He opened his eyes and turned around. Coach Walker was standing in the doorway of his bedroom.

"Going to miss you, Bron," he said. "But you know this isn't goodbye. You're still family and will always be family. Little Frankie's going to miss having you around so much, though. We all will. Now let's flip things around. You stay with us over the weekends."

LeBron liked that a lot. He felt an urge to eat Pam's German chocolate cake. He loved her cooking—the great pies she baked and everything she put on his plate.

"But it's all good," Frank continued. "This is the way it should be. You and your mama finally together in your own place. It's what we've all been working for."

LeBron noticed that Frank was holding a printed piece of parchment paper in his hands. He pointed to it and said, "What's that?"

"Oh," Frank said slowly. "This is something that you left behind at our house. I was pretty sure you would want to keep this." He handed it to LeBron.

LeBron looked at it and a large smile crossed his face.

"Thanks!" he exclaimed.

Coach Walker was right. He would have been really upset if this had been lost. It was the citizenship award he had gotten in fifth grade for his perfect attendance record at Portage Path Elementary.

Coach Walker put his arm around LeBron and said, "Catch you later, son," and quietly left the room.

LeBron looked down at the award again and he suddenly knew exactly where he was going to put it.

As soon as he found a tack, it was going right next to his Michael Jordan poster.

Fear and Duct Tape

"I'm sorry," the elderly woman at the front door said. "I don't need any. But I wish you two young men luck."

She smiled and closed the door quietly, leaving LeBron and Sian on her front porch alone, holding a box of duct tape each.

They were selling tape to raise funds for the Shooting Stars. If they qualified for the AAU nationals in Salt Lake City, they would use the money to fly to the tournament instead of driving.

"Couldn't we be normal and sell candy or something?" Sian said, as he and LeBron walked to the next house, "People are looking at us like we're Freaks of the Week selling duct tape."

"I talked to Coach Dru about that," LeBron said

seriously. "He told me that we couldn't sell candy because he was afraid you'd eat it all before we got to the first house."

LeBron didn't crack a smile.

Sian looked angry and opened his mouth to speak, but LeBron interrupted before he could say anything, "Uhhh. You know what Coach Dru says about cursing!"

Sian shut his mouth. He pushed a laughing LeBron very hard instead.

It had been a year since the Florida tournament and the Shooting Stars were starting to really gel as a team. LeBron was getting more confident in his abilities. He still wasn't much interested in defense, but he was learning that it was an important part of the game and he worked harder on it. Little Dru was starting to develop a jump shot that was getting more and more accurate. Sian was learning to use that big body of his more effectively.

The Shooting Stars played well enough to qualify for the AAU under-12 championship tournament in Salt Lake. Thanks to hard work and duct tape, they were going to get another crack at a possible national championship.

Sian, Little Dru, and LeBron were sitting together in the car as Coach Dru drove all of them to the Akron/Canton airport to catch the flight to Salt Lake City. Sian and Little Dru had been goofing with each other the entire time, but LeBron remained quiet.

Little Dru chimed in, "What's up with you, Bron? You've hardly said anything."

LeBron remained silent. He was a little embarrassed and didn't know what to say to his friends. What would they think of him if he told them the truth? Would they laugh at him? Would they think he was a baby? The truth was, LeBron had never been in an airplane before and the prospect of flying scared him.

"Yeah, what's up?" Sian said to LeBron as he pushed him good-naturedly. "We're going to Salt Lake City to play in the tournament! C'mon, lighten up, bro! It's gonna be great!"

"Just thinking about the tournament, that's all." LeBron lied.

He tried to be brave and it worked—until the car pulled into the airport parking lot. Then it felt a lot like his heart was going to stop.

Inside the airport concourse, LeBron was trying hard to laugh and goof with his other teammates like there wasn't anything wrong while they waited for their flight. But it was unreal—like he was watching a movie of himself laughing and talking to his teammates. That guy looked like he was having fun, while the real LeBron just wanted to run away and hide.

When it was announced that it was time to board the flight, LeBron froze.

"C'mon, Bron," Little Dru said. He nudged LeBron in the direction of the boarding gate.

LeBron didn't remember much from the time he handed the attendant his ticket at the gate to the time the airplane started rolling down the runway, gaining speed for takeoff. Sian was sitting next to LeBron and noticed that he had a terrified look on his face.

He leaned toward LeBron and said, "Uhhh. You know what Coach Dru says about cursing!"

But LeBron wasn't thinking about cursing. His ears were hurting and the jet engines were roaring and the airplane was moving fast and he was up in the air in a giant tin can that was going to crash and he and everybody he knew was going to die.

He burst into tears and couldn't stop crying.

"Dang, Bron. It was just a joke!" Sian exclaimed.

But at that moment, LeBron couldn't hear or see anything because his ears were plugged up and tears blurred his vision. All he knew was that right now he hated Salt Lake City and he hated basketball. But most of all, he hated duct tape, which had made this nightmare possible.

When the flight finally landed, LeBron breathed a sigh of relief. He felt as if he hadn't breathed for four hours.

Fortunately, the tournament turned out to be a lot more fun for LeBron. Despite some fierce competition against intimidating teams, the Shooting Stars managed to come in 10th in the competition.

As the team was waiting in line to board the flight back home to Akron from Salt Lake City International Airport, Sian asked LeBron, "You cool now, Bron? You're not going freak on the flight home, right?"

"Don't know what you're talking about." LeBron snapped. "Flying ain't nothing."

"Riiiight," Sian replied, as they walked down the corridor together to catch the flight home.

The Fab Four

"Hey," Willie McGee said to LeBron in Coach Dru's living room.

"Hey," LeBron shot back.

Little Dru didn't say anything to either of them. He was feverishly trying to finish his homework. Coach Dru had told Little Dru it had better be done or he was leaving for practice without him.

The Shooting Stars had just qualified for the Under-13 AAU championship tournament and Willie had joined the team because his team, the Akron Athletics, had failed to qualify.

LeBron remembered him well. Whenever they played against the Athletics he was impressed with Willie's power and his moves.

When Sian met Willie at practice, he had been subdued and a little wary.

"What do you think?" LeBron asked Sian when they were out of earshot of Willie.

"We'll see," Sian answered.

During a one-on-one drill, Sian defended Willie. Willie made a fake to the left and a pivot to the right around Sian that left him standing still with his mouth open.

"Damn!" Sian cried.

Little Dru and LeBron laughed because they knew what was coming.

Coach Dru blew his whistle and yelled, "That'll be 10 pushups, Sian!"

"Aw, that ain't cursing, Coach!" Sian complained.

Sian shot a quick look at Willie and Willie just shrugged. Sian shook his head slowly and got down to start his pushups.

It didn't take long into that first practice for LeBron to see that Willie belonged on the Shooting Stars. He just fit. LeBron was already starting to feel that same court bond with Willie that he felt with

Little Dru and Sian. He was just surprised that it had happened so quickly.

There was something about Willie that LeBron liked. Sure, he respected Willie's basketball skills, but there was more to it than that. He couldn't quite put his finger on it, but it was almost like there was a grownup living inside of his Willie's kid body. He projected a quiet confidence that LeBron appreciated.

LeBron invited Willie to come over his Spring Hill apartment to hang out with him, Little Dru, and Sian. Little Dru and Sian hadn't arrived yet, so LeBron and Willie were hanging out in LeBron's room until the other two boys arrived. Willie looked at the poster of Michael Jordan that LeBron had tacked to his wall.

"Man, I love MJ. But you have to love MJ if you're from Chicago," Willie said.

"I didn't know you're from Chicago!" LeBron exclaimed. "You ever get to see Michael play?"

Willie shook his head, "Naw. Never had the money to go to a game."

"So why'd your family move to Akron?" LeBron asked.

Willie hesitated, then answered softly, "My family didn't move out here. I'm living with my brother and his fiancé. I wanted to come out here and live with him."

"Why?"

Willie paused, contemplating whether to answer the question.

"Um. My parents have some problems," he finally said. "Never knew when they were going to be home." Willie stopped to collect his thoughts. "My brother took me in during his last year of college over at Akron University. He made sure I went to school. He taught me what I know about basketball. He's why I'm here."

LeBron understood. The same way LeBron was *here* because the Walkers and Coach Dru had lent a helping hand.

LeBron had sensed that Willie and he were alike in many ways. Willie had seen things and been through things that no kid should go through, and despite that he had come out strong.

There was a knock on the apartment door.

"C'mon, Willie," LeBron said. "Sian and Little Dru are here."

As he and Willie went to the door to let Sian and Little Dru into the apartment, LeBron was convinced of one thing: *Willie's one of us.*

Little Dru and Sian would figure that out soon enough, if they hadn't figured it out already.

They would be the Fab Four from now on. He opened the door to let his other brothers inside.

The Final Shot

LeBron was ready to win the championship. Last year they had all the pieces to make a deep run in the Under-13 tournament. They had added Willie to the lineup; Sian was a much better player; and Little Dru had become a dangerous force from the outside. But they had let it all slip through their fingers. They had spent more time in the motel swimming pool than focusing on playing basketball.

This year they wanted to redeem themselves.

After years of trying, they had finally reached the AAU Under-14 finals at the Wide World of Sports Complex in Orlando. They were getting ready to play against a team from Southern California that had won the championship for the past three years running.

You could tell the SoCal All-Stars thought they had it in the bag. Who were these nobodies from Akron, Ohio, who thought they could stay on the court with them? They weren't alone in thinking that; almost everyone at the tournament agreed that the SoCal All-Stars were going to wipe the court with the Northeast Ohio Shooting Stars. The only question that really remained was how much the Shooting Stars were going to lose by.

LeBron, Sian, Little Dru, and Willie watched the All Stars laugh and joke during pre-game warm-ups. It was obvious that they were not taking the game or the Shooting Stars seriously.

"Look at them," Little Dru spat near half-court. "They think we're just a bunch of punks."

"Yeah," Sian piped in. "Them and their fancy red Nike uniforms. Bunch of arrogant Hollywood movie star wannabes."

"Let 'em keep laughing," LeBron said. "We'll see who's laughing at the end of the game."

But the SoCal All-Stars were intimidating. They had a couple of players who topped out at 6 feet

5 inches and they were a good team. But LeBron felt that he wasn't just playing for himself; he was playing for the entire city of Akron. He wanted the world to know that Akron was a place to be reckoned with.

Before tip-off, Coach Dru called them into a huddle on the sideline.

He looked at each and every one of them and said, "This is about a journey. We've played together, we've fought together, and we are going to win or lose together. We've gotten this far and you've beaten a lot of good teams to get here."

He hesitated, then continued, "I know you can do this. You know you can do this if you play your game. But, regardless of the outcome, know that I am proud of you."

"Now, put your hands in and let them hear in Akron who you are!"

The team shouted, "Shooting Stars!" so loudly that that some people in Akron might have heard it.

The game was not going well for the Shooting Stars.

The Southern California All-Stars were making it look easy. They were grabbing offensive boards for easy second-chance buckets and were scoring at will on fast breaks. At half time, the Shooting Stars were down by 15 points.

In the locker room, LeBron was angry and frustrated. He didn't have to look at Little Dru, Sian, and Willie to know that they felt the same way. LeBron knew, deep down, that they were better than what they had shown on the court in the first half. They just weren't playing together as a team and were letting the All Stars dictate the action.

They were sitting next to each other when LeBron leaned in and whispered angrily, "Is this how we're going to go down?"

"The All Stars are laughing at us. They're laughing at Akron."

They all knew LeBron was right. They had all talked about going to the finals and becoming champions for years. This was their last chance to do it together before they all went to high school. They were in the finals—a heartbeat away from their dream—and they were letting it slip from their grasp.

LeBron looked at Willie, Little Dru, and Sian and said, "I'm not going down like this. That's a fact."

"Damn straight," Sian whispered, afraid to say it too loud for fear of pushups.

Willie said nothing, but he never had to. You could see his answer in his eyes.

"Then let's go out and do this," LeBron said.

The second half was a different story. The SoCal All-Stars couldn't stop Willie from crashing the boards and making key offensive and defensive rebounds. Sian suddenly became an immovable force that clamped down on the All-Star's inside game. Little Dru was using the jump shot he had developed to hit buckets from the outside and kept the All-Stars from constantly keying on LeBron. LeBron was all over the court, hitting baskets from the outside, driving into traffic to make easy layups and draw fouls, and finding open teammates to feed the ball when he was double-teamed.

The smug looks that the All Stars had on their faces during the first half were replaced by concerned looks after the Shooting Stars closed the scoring gap by ten points, then five points, then down to one point.

With little time left and down by one point, LeBron saw an open lane to the basket. He drove hard to the hoop and went up.

Should I go for the dunk?

At the last moment, he changed his mind, deciding to go for the lay-in.

And the shot was blocked!

Hurriedly, the Shooting Stars fouled a SoCal player, who missed the first free throw and made the second.

Down by two, with four seconds to go, a timeout was called.

When Coach Dru called the play, LeBron knew it was going to be up to him. A three-pointer would win it. The dream was on his shoulders. All the hard work, all of the tears, and all of the years together would come down to this last moment. And he would only get one chance.

The ball was inbounded to LeBron. He dribbled once and with one second left he shot a three-pointer from 35 feet. He watched the trajectory of the ball as it headed toward the basket. It was as if all of the air had been sucked out of the building as the ball sailed closer to the hoop. You could hear a pin drop.

LeBron held his breath as the ball hit the rim, rattled around...

And popped out.

The SoCal All-Stars had just won the championship game by two points.

LeBron sat down as the SoCal All-Stars started celebrating around him. He felt like he had let down his brothers and his team and the entire city of Akron. He began to cry and didn't think he would ever stop.

A Surprise Move

Little Dru had called them to meet him at McDonald's. "I'm going to St. V," he announced to LeBron, Sian, and Willie, who all looked shocked.

Going to St. Vincent-St. Mary? This was astonishing news, to say the least.

LeBron asked "Why St. V? I thought we decided we were going to stick together and go to Buchtel."

Little Dru thought for a moment, then replied, "They're not going to give me a chance to play varsity at Buchtel. Besides, all Buchtel really wants is you, Bron. We all know that."

"Coach Dambrot is going to be head varsity coach at St. V this year," Little Dru continued. "I think he'll give me a fair shot. He actually wants me to be on his team."

That didn't surprise LeBron. He knew Keith
Dambrot. Little Dru and LeBron had been going
to his basketball clinics at the Jewish Community
Center for a while.

This was a problem. After the loss to the SoCal
All-Stars, the four of them had vowed that they
would go to the same high school and play together.

"So," Willie said. "Looks like we have a decision
to make."

Everybody at the table knew what that meant.
Would they stay together and follow Little Dru to
St. V instead of going to Buchtel?

LeBron knew exactly what the black community
in Akron would be saying about them. A group
of black basketball players snubbing a public high
school that was the pride of the black community in
Akron in favor of attending a mostly white private
Catholic school? They'd be labeled sellouts and
probably worse. Traitors.

Also LeBron had never hung out much with
white people in Akron. How would he fit in at a
mostly white school? How would any of them fit

in? Would they ever be accepted or would they always be considered outsiders who were brought in as hired guns to take over St. V's basketball program?

The thought of going to St. V scared him a bit. It was risky and it wasn't going to be easy. He would be stepping from the known solidly into the unknown.

"We have to stick together," LeBron finally said to the group. "I think we need to see it through, like we said."

"I'm in," Willie said curtly.

Sian chimed in, "Who's gonna keep Little Dru from making a fool of himself if I'm not there to bail him out?"

LeBron looked directly at Little Dru. "Hey, isn't the mascot at St. V a fighting leprechaun? Are you sure they want you to play basketball for them or did they just need somebody who could fit into the leprechaun suit?"

Little Dru threw a french fry at LeBron and they all started laughing.

So it was decided. The Fab Four would stay together. They would all go to St. V and play for Coach Dambrot, come what may. They might even lose friends over their decision. But their real friends and their families would always support them. And being together was all that really mattered. They had some history to make, the four of them.

LeBron was sure of it.

What Happened?

As LeBron had predicted, the four friends took a lot of heat for their decision, but they stuck to it and enrolled at St. Vincent-St. Mary.

After their first basketball practice, LeBron was seriously wondering if they had made the right decision. Sian was too angry to speak. Little Dru could only shake his head. Willie looked calm and collected on the outside, but LeBron knew that he had to be upset, too.

What had happened to the nice Coach Dambrot who had been so helpful and understanding at the basketball clinics? Nothing they were doing was good enough. They were all worthless freshmen who thought they knew the game. They didn't even understand the basic fundamentals of basketball.

They were wasting his time, St. Vincent's time, and the team's time. LeBron was convinced that the Coach Dambrot from the Jewish Community Center had been replaced by a fire-breathing maniac.

They were only 14-year-old kids, but Coach Dambrot was treating them like they were Division 1 college players. And LeBron suspected that Coach Dambrot could easily make grown college players run home crying to their mamas.

He had the terrible feeling that all of them had made a huge mistake coming to St. Vincent to play basketball. Maverick Carter, who was a senior and the team captain, met the group outside the gym after practice was over. LeBron had known Maverick since he was five, so he respected his opinion.

"What is up with that guy, Mav?" LeBron asked.

Maverick looked at the angry friends and said, "I don't know, Bron. It's his style. But if you give him time, he's going to make all of us better basketball players. Just keep your heads low and I'll try to give you some cover. Life isn't easy for freshmen."

Maverick walked away, leaving the four fuming friends to talk amongst themselves.

Sian was furious. "First we gotta put up with this school and its dress code and its stupid rules and white kids staring at us all day and now we gotta put up with Freddie from Nightmare on Elm Street for a basketball coach? Buchtel isn't looking so bad to me right about now."

Willie, as always, was the level-headed one. "It is what it is. We're here now. Yeah, he's tough, but if we go back to Buchtel now, everybody is going to be all like, 'I told you so.'"

Willie looked at Little Dru and Sian. "Besides, both of your dads are assistant coaches for the team now. If we up and quit, it's going to make them look bad, too," he said.

They all nodded reluctantly.

LeBron knew that what Willie was saying was true, but he was still angry. It seemed like Coach Dambrot had singled him out for the most abuse.

During the practice he was always on him. Even when he did things right, it was wrong. And when he did things wrong... well, God help him if he did something wrong.

Inside the gym, a different conversation was going on.

"Weren't you a little hard on those boys?" Coach Dru said to Keith Dambrot.

Coach Dambrot chuckled. "Maybe. But I have to be hard on them. We have talent, but talent only takes you so far. I've seen teams with all the talent in the world go nowhere because they had no discipline."

Coach Dru nodded. He understood that, but he had been shocked by Coach Dambrot's tactics. Coach Dru was as quiet and soft-spoken as Coach Dambrot was fiery and loud.

"I noticed you were really tough on LeBron. I know that boy and he was pretty angry at you," Coach Dru said.

Coach Dambrot thought for a moment and then spoke, "Between you and me, that kid is the best

14-year-old player I've ever seen. I've coached three players who went on to play in the NBA and if that kid stays healthy, he's going pro. I have no doubt about it."

He leaned in toward Coach Dru and said quietly, "But it's up to us to make sure all of that talent is channeled properly and he doesn't get a big head."

"I get it," Coach Dru replied. "Oh and one other thing. I don't want you to take offense, but about all that cursing during practice…"

"What cursing?" Coach Dambrot said with a wink.

Throughout that freshman season, Coach Dambrot didn't let up and St. Vincent's Fighting Irish basketball team didn't stop winning. The team found that playing in games was easy compared to the practices. LeBron sometimes thought playing in a war zone was probably easier than practices, but he had also grudgingly accepted that he had become a far better player under Coach Dambrot's tough love. He was a starter and Willie, Sian, and Little Dru usually came in for support off the bench.

With Maverick Carter's leadership, they had gelled into a very good team.

At the end of the season, the Fighting Irish had finished with a perfect record and had won all of their playoffs games, which led to the Division III championship game against Jamestown's Greenview High School at Value City Arena at Ohio State University.

The crowd of over 13,000 was about to witness one of the most amazing feats in Ohio high school basketball championship history.

"Dru, get in there!" Coach Dambrot yelled, pointing toward the timer's table.

The game was close and the Irish were behind in the first quarter. Coach Dambrot was worried. Greenview had slowed down the game and was playing tough zone defense. He needed somebody in the game who could gun from the outside and open it up.

When Little Dru ran onto the court you could hear the laughter scattered among the crowd. His basketball shorts went past his knees and he was all of 5 feet tall and about 100 pounds.

People started chanting, "Ball Boy!"

LeBron greeted Little Dru at the top of the key. He knew that Little Dru could hear the laughter, but he also knew that it only made him stronger and more determined to prove everybody wrong.

"Ready to do this?" LeBron asked.

Little Dru nodded, but said nothing. When play resumed, he got fed the ball in the corner behind the three-point line. He had an open look and he didn't hesitate to take the shot. Three!

The next shot Little Dru took was about two feet behind the three-point line in the other corner. All net. Three!

But Little Dru wasn't done. It was like he was possessed. LeBron had played with Little Dru enough to see when he was in the zone. LeBron was having a good game, but he also knew when it was time to feed the ball to the hot player.

The ball was passed to LeBron at the top of the key, but rather than drive to the basket, he immediately passed it to Little Dru who was waiting in the left corner behind the three-point line. The defender tried to block the shot, but Little Dru was too quick. Never any doubt. Three!

This is crazy, LeBron thought.

Little Dru swished *another* three-pointer before he was taken out of the game near the end of the first half. That basket gave St. Vincent the lead, 27-25. At the half time break, LeBron wouldn't even look at Little Dru. He didn't want to jinx him.

And it worked, because in the second half, Little Dru tossed in *three more* three-pointers. All in all, he had thrown up seven threes and had made all seven, which tied a playoff record. He had played just 10 minutes in the championship game and had scored 21 points to help lead the Irish to a 73-55 victory over Greenview.

Nobody was laughing at Little Dru anymore.

After the game, LeBron grabbed Little Dru and hoisted him into the air.

"We did it! You did it! You showed them!" LeBron yelled. He felt like a proud big brother.

LeBron was happy. He looked proudly at his teammates as they all took turns hoisting the championship trophy above their heads. It was so big that Little Dru had trouble lifting it when it was his turn.

They had won a state championship together. And with that championship came vindication for the decision they had made to attend St. Vincent, despite the criticism that had been leveled against them. It had been a tough road, but it had been worth it.

But LeBron knew, deep down, that one championship wasn't going to be enough.

Legacy

"How are we going to beat Oak Hill if you can't play defense, LeBron!" Coach Dambrot yelled at him during practice. "Oh my God! They are going to kill us!"

LeBron thought that maybe Coach Dambrot was going to be easier on him now that he was a sophomore. It turned out he had been wildly mistaken.

Everybody who knew anything about high school basketball knew about Oak Hill Academy in Virginia. They had been a basketball powerhouse for years and were consistently ranked as one of the top 10 high school basketball teams in the country. After winning the Ohio Division III championship in 2000, St. Vincent-St. Mary had been ranked 21st in the nation. This year, it appeared that Coach

Dambrot had even bigger plans for them. He had scheduled St. V to play against several of the top 25 high school basketball teams from around the country.

LeBron knew that people in Akron expected St. V to win another Ohio State Division III championship this year. But Maverick Carter had graduated and the team was looking to LeBron for leadership. It was a big responsibility for a 15-year-old kid. But he felt he was up to it. That is, if he survived another year under Coach Dambrot's withering criticism.

This is what he had always wanted. His goal wasn't to win just another state championship, but to win a *national championship*. That dream went back to when he was a little kid and had started playing for the Shooting Stars. The longing to put Akron on the map was fueled even more by the Shooting Stars close loss to the SoCal All-Stars just two years earlier. They had been only *three points* away from an AAU national title and *he* had missed the buzzer-beating winning shot.

It still hurt.

Their sophomore season started where their freshman season had left off. They were posting easy wins against in-state and out-of-state opponents, winning by 30 to 40 points in some games. They were 9-0 when they finally met Oak Hill Academy.

The battle between the two schools had turned into a thrilling back and forth game with neither team giving in to the other. LeBron was putting on a show; nailing threes, driving to the basket for dunks, and making spectacular passes.

There was a man in the stands who really liked what he saw. His name was Jerry Krause and he was the general manager of the Chicago Bulls. He had come to the game to check out a couple of players on the Oak Hill squad, but instead found himself more and more impressed with a kid on the St. Vincent-St. Mary team he hadn't even come to see play. Where had he been hiding? How could his scouts have missed this kid?

"Who is that number 23 from St. Vincent?

How come I've never heard of him?" he asked his assistant.

His assistant scrambled to find his program. "Some kid named LeBron James," he answered. "And check this out, he's only a sophomore."

"What?" Krause exclaimed. He couldn't believe it. This kid was only 15 and was outplaying everybody on the court. How good would he be when he was a *senior?*

Krause whistled. "We need to keep an eye on this kid!"

Despite LeBron's amazing game, and the entire team's outstanding effort, St. V ended up losing to Oak Hill 79-78.

After the game, LeBron cried. He had missed a difficult 25-foot shot at the buzzer that could have won the game for the Irish. To him, it was the SoCal All-Star game all over again. He had the final look and he had missed. He had blown it and St. V's chances for a national championship this year were over.

In between the tears, he tried to console himself.

At least we know we can hang with the best, he thought.

St. Vincent did not lose another game during the regular season and won the Division III championship again, defeating Casstown East Miami 65-53. On the bus ride home after the game, the team was celebrating their back-to-back championships. They were kings. At least for today. Even Coach Dambrot looked pleased.

"Three-Peat!" Sian yelled.

Everybody was laughing and goofing.

"Next year we take it all!" LeBron screamed.

He felt it in his bones. This season was done and next season was going to be a season of destiny.

Fame

While excelling in basketball, LeBron was also
playing football and was named to the Ohio Division
IV All-State first team as a wide receiver. Big time
college football powers were starting to look at him.
LeBron loved playing football, but he knew, deep
down, that basketball was his true calling.

At the end of St. V's basketball season last year
it seemed like his bedroom wasn't going to be large
enough to hold all the honors he received. He was
named the Sporting News' Sophomore Basketball
Player of the Year. And when it was announced
that he would be the first sophomore ever to
receive the prestigious Mr. Basketball award given
to the best high school basketball player in Ohio, he
thought his mama was going to have a heart attack.

She started jumping up and down and screaming at 602 Spring Hill, making so much noise that a couple of neighbors rushed over to see what the commotion was about.

"My baby is the best high school basketball player in Ohio, that's all," she told them proudly. "So I hope you don't mind if I scream some more." Then she did.

When he was the first sophomore ever named to the *USA Today* All-USA First Team, the kid from Akron became news outside of Ohio. Suddenly, he couldn't go anywhere in Akron without somebody asking for his autograph.

"Are you the guy I'm supposed to be getting an autograph from?" a waitress had asked at a local restaurant he was eating at. He had to smile. She didn't know who he was, but the guys working in the kitchen certainly did. People were treating him like he was a rock star and it was hard not to feel that way with people stopping him wherever he went to get his autograph or take a picture with him. He had even met his favorite rapper, Jay-Z, in

Chicago. During the offseason, LeBron had been invited to play in elite basketball tournaments where he got to face off against the best high school players in the country. When he bested some of the best in the nation, it just added to his growing fame. Adidas and Nike were battling to get LeBron to wear their shoes and their clothes. Adidas even made a shoe with LeBron's name and number on it.

Then a dream came true. During the summer, he had been the only high school player among college players and pros invited to participate in a private workout session with Michael Jordan. Michael Jordan! His idol! When LeBron and his mama finally met MJ in person, he was so nervous he could barely speak. He thought he might pass out. It was unreal. He wanted to jump up and down like he was a nine-year-old Shooting Star again.

As usual, Mama was at no loss for words. She said to MJ, "You're going to take good care of my Bron, right?"

Michael had smiled. MJ got along just fine with LeBron and Mama after that.

But he was a junior now and it was time to buckle down and get to business. He was 6'8" and about 200 pounds and was feeling stronger and more confident than ever. This season he felt like nobody would be able to stop him on the court. Nobody.

People were saying he was good enough to be an NBA player right now. They were comparing him to Kobe Bryant and Magic Johnson. Part of him thought that was ridiculous, but another part of him was saying, what if?

LeBron noticed that even the kids at St. V were looking at him differently as he made his way down the hallway at school. It was almost like they were in awe of him. Like he was a celebrity walking down the red carpet. LeBron had to admit, he liked the attention. He liked it a lot.

He was almost to math class when a fellow student yelled, "Hail, King James!"

LeBron smiled and waved mockingly to the kid in a fancy way he thought a king might wave from a balcony and everybody laughed. LeBron may have made a joke about it, but he felt that it wasn't too far from the truth. He was the king of high school basketball right now. At least in Ohio.

King James, he thought. *I'm going to have to start using that.*

St. V had added Romeo Travis to the team. He was hard to get along with, but he was also a very good player. With Romeo, Willie, Sian, and Little Dru on the team this year, there was going to be no stopping them. They were destined for the state championship, even though they had been moved up to Division II. LeBron had never lost to an Ohio high school basketball team and he didn't plan on losing to one this year.

St. V had also been scheduled to play some of the best teams in the nation again, including Oak Hill Academy. They would be flying all over the country just like the pros. All the pieces were in place. This was going to be an epic year and King James was set to rule over his basketball kingdom. It was hard not to let all of this stuff go to his head, but he couldn't help but feel that everything was possible for him and the Fab Four this year.

Not Alone

When LeBron first heard the news from Little Dru, he didn't believe it. But Little Dru had heard the news directly from his father, and Coach Dru would never make up something like this.

So, it was true. Coach Dambrot was leaving St. Vincent-St. Mary to take a coaching job at the University of Akron!

The Fab Four were gathered at LeBron's apartment to talk about the shocking news. LeBron looked over at Little Dru and could see the look of deep hurt in his eyes. He had been closer to Coach Dambrot than any of them. The sad expression on Little Dru's face made LeBron even angrier at Coach Dambrot.

"I'm done with him," LeBron said angrily. "How can he do this to us?"

"My Dad had to hear the news from a reporter," Little Dru said quietly.

They had signed on to St. V to play for Coach Dambrot and had taken a lot of heat from their community for doing that. There was an unspoken pact that they would see this through all together. This was going to be the year when they had it all: a state and a national championship. The dream was within their grasp. But Coach Dambrot had just left them abandoned on the side of the road in the middle of their journey. Now what were they going to do?

Coach Dambrot asked Coach Dru to take over for him and Coach Dru reluctantly stepped into his large shoes. He had always wanted to be a high school basketball head coach; he just never expected that his first high school head coaching job would be for a team that had only lost one game in two years, was ranked in the top 10 in the nation, and was anchored by one of the best high school players in the United States.

St. V basketball games had become so popular last season that the school administration decided to move home games to the University of Akron's Rhodes Arena to accommodate the mobs. Coach Dru would be coaching in a fishbowl and every mistake he made would be magnified in front of large crowds and then reported on the front page of every sports section in Ohio.

But he couldn't say no. He had coached the Fab Four since they were little kids playing for the Shooting Stars and they trusted him. He decided he'd give it a go.

Coach Dru was giving instructions to the team during practice, but LeBron wasn't listening. Coach Dru was like family and he didn't fear him the way he had Coach Dambrot. He had been arguing more with Coach Dru this season, and sometimes he did what he wanted to do during games despite what Coach Dru told him. But they were still winning. So who cared whether they disrespected Coach Dru at times and were fighting amongst themselves?

That's what family did sometimes. LeBron was putting up impressive numbers, so he could pick and choose when he wanted to follow Coach Dru's instructions. He was King James and people were saying that this team was so good they could probably win it all without a coach.

LeBron didn't entirely disagree with that.

They had already beaten Germantown Academy, which had been ranked sixth in the nation and then had turned around and defeated seventh-ranked Vashon High School out of St. Louis. They had beaten top teams from Detroit and New Jersey. And, as usual, Ohio teams were just a joke. Another win? Ho hum. Who's next?

Coach Dru had harped that they weren't playing up to their potential and were losing their edge. He said they had been outright lucky to win some of those games. LeBron thought Coach Dru worried too much. A win was still a win. When the game was on the line, they always pulled through.

Just chill, Coach, LeBron thought. *This is our year.*

The Circus Comes to Town

At 17, LeBron already had the media game down, so when *Sports Illustrated* magazine said they would be interested in doing a story about him and if he wouldn't mind if a reporter tagged around with him for a few days, it wasn't a big deal to him. He'd been interviewed for more articles than he could remember. They asked if they could do a photo shoot, too.

So when the reporter arrived at St. V in early February, LeBron just took the whole thing in stride. The reporter followed him during practice and around school and went with him as he watched a Cleveland Cavaliers versus the Chicago Bulls game at Gund Arena in Cleveland that night. LeBron even got to meet Michael Jordan after the game.

Michael's first question to LeBron was, "Where's Mama?"

LeBron couldn't help but laugh.

The next day, the reporter had a photographer and an assistant in tow to take shots of LeBron in the St. V gym. The rest of the Fab Four couldn't resist being there to watch the shoot. Things went fine until the photographer started spraying LeBron's face and arms with water to make him look like he was sweating. Sian hooted, "More than I've seen you sweat all year!"

LeBron cringed. *This is ridiculous,* he thought. *When is this going to be over?*

After the shoot, the reporter sat down with LeBron and told him, "We're going to run you on the cover."

LeBron smiled and shrugged. "That's cool," he said nonchalantly. He had been on magazine covers before, so how big a deal could this really be? Nobody he knew in his neighborhood actually read *Sports Illustrated.*

"Only cool?" the reporter said. "Do you realize that only three other high school basketball players in the history of *Sports Illustrated* have been on the cover?"

"Really?"

"Really," the reporter replied. "And you'll be the first high school *junior* on the cover, ever."

LeBron had to admit that was *very* cool. Would it change his life? He doubted it. How much crazier could a *Sports Illustrated* cover story make his already crazy life? Not much, he wagered.

After the LeBron issue hit the stands, he found out how much crazier his life could get. Apparently, a few people outside of his neighborhood *did* read *Sports Illustrated.* The cover showed him holding a golden basketball in his right hand, his left arm stretched toward the camera. He was looking straight ahead. His mouth was forming an "O," like he was daring the reader to try to stop him.

The headline read: THE CHOSEN ONE. The caption under the headline read: *High school junior LeBron James would be an NBA lottery pick right now.*

As LeBron read the article at home, he couldn't believe it. It said he could be the next *Michael Jordan.* It was flattering and ridiculous at the same time. He was only a junior in high school. How could they compare him to the greatest player of all time? The article went on to quote a couple of NBA general managers who said that if they could, they would take him in the first round—*this year.*

As the days wore on, LeBron found himself inundated with people holding the LeBron James *Sports Illustrated* issue for him to sign. Some people brought stacks of magazines with them. LeBron felt obligated to sign them all, until he found out that the autographed magazines were finding their way to eBay. When he started saying no, adults would have their kids approach him to sign the magazines.

He couldn't go anywhere now without at least a dozen people calling out, "Hey, Chosen One!" Sports agents were approaching his friends and family, handing them manila envelopes and saying, "Would you mind handing this to LeBron?"

St. Vincent-St. Mary had to officially ban

reporters and news crews from campus to keep them from interfering with classes and practices. The school had to hire a media consultant just to handle all of the interview requests. Even his own mother had gotten into the act.

"Maybe you should seriously think about trying to go pro after this season, Bron," she said to him one morning at breakfast. "Now would be the time, with the *Sports Illustrated* article and all. People will be falling all over themselves to get you to play for them."

Getting the money and helping to get Mama out of 602 Spring Hill and into a nice place in a nice neighborhood was always on his mind. She deserved better. And they *had* already discussed the possibility of petitioning the NBA to let him declare for the draft at the end of this season. But right now, he was in the middle of this high school basketball season and it was too early to think about that.

Besides, he had made a promise to Sian, Little Dru, and Willie that he would see it through to the end with them. Even if he could go pro, leaving would be a betrayal of their trust. It would be breaking up the Fab Four. That just couldn't happen.

Not yet, anyway.

It All Blows Up

When St. V met their nemesis Oak Hill
Academy in LeBron's junior year, the game was
played in Trenton, New Jersey, at the Sovereign
Bank Arena. Oak Hill was rated number one in
the nation again. The venue was crowded with
pro and college scouts who had come to watch
the duel between LeBron and Oak Hill star,
Carmelo Anthony.

And they didn't disappoint. LeBron threw in 36
points that night and Carmelo was just behind him
with 34 points. In the end, Oak Hill proved to be
too strong and St. V fell to them 72-66.

"Good game, Melo," LeBron said to Carmelo
after the final buzzer had sounded. They knew
each other and had become friends when they had

roomed together during an off-season tournament the year before.

Carmelo smiled. "How's it feel to be game MVP?"

LeBron shook his head slowly, "How's it feel to school us and knock us out of contention again? Don't you guys ever get tired of beating us?"

Carmelo thought for a moment and then said seriously. "No."

They both laughed, hugged briefly, and Carmelo headed to Oak Hill's locker room.

LeBron stood alone on the court for a moment. He hated losing, but he wasn't all that upset that St. V had lost. It wasn't like after last year's game against Oak Hill, when he had been crying and devastated by their loss. The dream of a national championship was over for this season, but they were still undefeated in league play. They'd just go out and run the rest of the season and win their third straight state championship. As far as LeBron was concerned, there was nobody left on their schedule that could beat them.

Although they had lost three games to out-of-state teams during the regular season, no basketball team from Ohio had beat them. And once again, St. V found itself in familiar territory: heading to Columbus to play the state championship at the Value City Arena for the third consecutive year.

It was three o'clock in the morning the day of the championship game and LeBron and Little Dru were listening to Jay-Z in their Columbus hotel room and goofing. LeBron wasn't worried that they were still up. They had stayed up just as late before other games and had won them. They were facing Roger Bacon for the championship, and they had beaten Roger Bacon this season already. So why worry?

Yes, Coach Dru had come out of his room and lectured the entire team about being up late and not being committed and taking this game for granted. And yes, they had nodded and said, "Yes, Coach. We'll go to sleep now." And then they had turned down the music and kept goofing anyway. Who needed sleep? St. V would take care of business tonight. LeBron had said in a press conference that he wouldn't let his team lose and he meant it. Coach Dru didn't understand they had this game in the bag.

So he and Little Dru went right on partying like they had already won the game.

A record crowd of over 18,000 people watched as Roger Bacon battled tough. They were acting like they weren't afraid of St. V at all. The lead kept changing back and forth.

At half-time, Roger Bacon led 31-30. And it was more of the same in the second half. Roger Bacon was not going away. LeBron had assumed they would cave by now, but the lead kept changing hands.

He was doing all he could to keep St. V in the game, but it was hard. His back hurt, Little Dru was missing shots, they were being outmuscled at the rim, they were making bad decisions on the court, and the referees were calling the game close.

The crowd was roaring, sensing upset.

The crowd is against us, LeBron thought. *They want us to lose.*

With less than 20 seconds remaining, Roger
Bacon was ahead, 66-63.

No need to panic, LeBron thought. *There's
plenty of time. We've been in this situation dozens
of times and have pulled it out. Just have to stay
cool. Be cool.*

LeBron got the inbound pass, but didn't dish
off the ball to Little Dru for a possible tying three.
Instead, he passed it off to an open teammate who
missed the open look from the corner. A Roger
Bacon player got the rebound and was immediately
fouled with nine seconds left.

Then LeBron watched in horror as Little Dru
grabbed the ball and *threw* it against the backboard.

A technical foul was whistled.

LeBron looked at Little Dru in disbelief. What
had he just done? Now Roger Bacon had two
shots coming on the foul, plus a two-shot technical
and *then* they would get possession of the ball
again. It would be a miracle if St. V could pull it
out now.

LeBron grabbed Little Dru by the jersey.

"What have you done?" he yelled. "We still had time!"

Little Dru didn't look at him, because he knew exactly what he had done.

It felt like time was running in slow motion to LeBron as the final buzzer sounded. Instead of celebrating his third consecutive state championship, LeBron watched as the Roger Bacon players celebrated their 69-63 upset victory over St. Vincent-St. Mary.

He looked at Coach Dru and could see the quiet pain in his expression. He looked into the crowd and saw his mama crying. He had let down the people he loved because he had let all the fame and success go to his head. They had believed that nobody could beat them and that they didn't have to work hard and now what did they have? No national championship. No state championship.

Nothing.

There would be time for anger, regrets, and sadness later, but right now LeBron knew one thing for certain: Things were going to have to change.

Destiny

The loss to Roger Bacon still stung. LeBron had a bitter taste in his mouth about it that wouldn't go away. Most teams would have been happy with a four-loss season, but they were St. V and everybody expected more of them. More importantly, they expected more of themselves.

They had let the dream slip through their fingers. And it had been their fault. They had disrespected Coach Dru and they had argued amongst themselves. They had deserved to lose. LeBron received a second-straight Mr. Basketball award, but he would have traded that in a heartbeat for a second chance to make the season right.

It was a new school year and a new basketball season. They were seniors now and it would be their last chance to realize the dream of winning a national championship and a state championship together. It was time to grow up. LeBron had even decided not to play football his senior season, so he could concentrate on basketball alone.

The Fab Four plus Romeo gathered in the St. V locker room before their first basketball practice.

"*USA Today's* preseason poll just came out," LeBron said to his friends. "They ranked us 23rd in the country. Twenty-third! They think we're done."

LeBron hesitated for a moment, then continued, "And if we act like we did last year, they're right. We *are* done."

He looked at his friends. He didn't have to say anything more about that. They all knew it was true.

LeBron continued, "We need to change. We rise or we fall together."

He hesitated and then spoke directly to Romeo. "And Romeo, you are one of us now. From now on we're the Fab *Five*."

He stood and put his hand up in the air. The others gathered around and joined hands with him.

"1, 2, 3. We're Ready! We're Squad!" he shouted.

"We're Ready! We're Squad!" they all shouted together, loud enough for the whole country to hear.

They started out the season as good as their word. St. Vincent-St. Mary destroyed local teams and had already beaten three teams ranked in the nation's top 10. At 7-0, St. V had gone from a ranking of 23rd in the nation to 5th in the nation. They had flown to Los Angeles to play against #4 Mater Dei at UCLA's Pauley Pavilion. They were in the house of Coach John Wooden.

LeBron had a terrible game, but Willie, Little Dru, and Romeo filled in the gaps and St. V defeated Mater Dei, 64-58. The win had been especially sweet since many of the players on Mater Dei had been on the same SoCal All-Stars squad that had beaten the Shooting Stars in the Under-14 AAU national championship game.

It had all come full circle. And the feeling of destiny was strong.

After beating Mater Dei, St. V was rated #1 in the nation by *USA Today.* Throughout the season, LeBron kept up his relentless pursuit to keep them there. He was averaging 31 points per game. They kept their undefeated streak going throughout league play and into the playoffs. And suddenly it all came down to one game. Everything was on the line. The state championship. The national championship. The dream.

St. V was in Columbus again for the Division II championship game. LeBron had learned his lesson the hard way last year. They were going to play Kettering Alter for the Division II championship. And yes, they had destroyed Kettering Alter by 33 points just three weeks earlier during the regular season. But hadn't St. V beaten Roger Bacon in the regular season last year before the championship game, too? How did that turn out?

There was no partying or staying up all night at the hotel the night before the game. On the bus ride over to the Value City Arena, there was no laughing and no goofing. You could hear a pin drop inside the bus as it pulled up to the arena entrance for the game.

In the locker room before the tip-off, Coach Dru was writing plays on the dri-board and giving some last minute instructions. Suddenly, he put down the marker and turned to face them all.

"Enough of this. You know all this," he said softly. "From here on in, it's about heart."

LeBron sat quietly, looking at Little Dru, Sian, Willie, and Romeo. This was their last dance. He had known most of them since he was a scared kid wondering where he was going to sleep at night. They were more than teammates. They were family.

It made him happy that the dream was within their grasp and they all might be able to share it. But it was bittersweet. This was the last game of basketball they would ever play together. They had started in a beat-up, little Salvation Army gym and now here they all were, still together. Where had the years gone? They had flown by and now all of the tears and laughter and wins and losses and untold hours of practice and travel now boiled down to 32 minutes of playing time.

LeBron didn't have to ask if the other members of the Fab Five were thinking the same thing. He knew they were. He thought about Coach Dru. This would be LeBron's last game playing for him. He was like a father to LeBron. Coach Dru didn't have to take him under his wing and buy him things and make him part of his family, but he had. He had pushed him, but he had also taught him that there was more to life than basketball. Basketball was only a means to an end. Winning wasn't about a score at the end of a game. It was about becoming the best man you could become.

They had all taken a long journey together, and one part of it would end tonight after the final buzzer sounded.

It was no surprise that Kettering Alter was not the same team St. V had faced three weeks before. Their new strategy was to slow things down. Way down.

Rather than taking quick shots, Alter passed the ball. And passed the ball. Then reset and passed the ball some more until they had a good look at the basket. They were hanging on to the ball until they found a shot they liked.

This was not the game St. V liked to play. The Irish were getting frustrated chasing Alter players around and were making errors on the floor trying to get them to pick up the pace. But Alter was disciplined and was not budging. The 20,000 people in the arena couldn't believe it. The team that had lost to St. V by 33 points just about a month ago went into halftime with a 19-14 lead.

In the locker room, nobody said a word, but everybody was thinking it. Could this be another upset? LeBron couldn't accept that. Their long journey together couldn't end in defeat. It just couldn't. He wouldn't let it.

Coach Dru looked at them all. He told the team that they had to stop relying on LeBron to win the game for them. They all needed to step up.

Coach Dru paused, "Look around the room. Hey,

let's be real about this. To be where you guys are is just a blessing that you will only understand later in life."

He shook his head slowly as he looked downward. "Let's just do this. Let's end this thing the right way."

LeBron stood up and said, "One. Two. Three."

And the rest of the room said, "Team!"

LeBron then said, "Four. Five. Six."

"Work hard," they said in unison.

And they all went back out to face whatever fate had in store for them.

In the second half, St. V immediately began putting a dent into Kettering Alter's lead. As the half wore on, the pressure defense that Coach Dru had ordered was rattling them. The discipline that Alter had shown in the first half was beginning to unravel and St. V was getting into their heads.

St. V also took to heart what Coach Dru had said about not relying on LeBron to win the game. Romeo caught fire and started scoring at will. Sian became a bulldog on defense, denying Alter players access to the basket. Little Dru held Alter's star player to zero points for most of the second half. With just three minutes left in the game, St. V found itself up by 10 points.

Kettering Alter made one last desperate push to win the game. A game that had been 38-28 with three minutes left to play had suddenly become a 40-36 game with 22 seconds to play. Alter still had a shot.

On the inbound, Alter got the ball to a player who had a good look for a three pointer from the corner. LeBron watched as the ball arced toward the basket. He drove in for the rebound. The ball bounced off the rim and LeBron grabbed it. He dribbled out and passed to Little Dru, who dribbled around until time expired.

St. V had won.

LeBron was smiling so hard he thought his face was going to break. He was jumping up and down.

He looked up at the arena seats and saw his mother running down the steps. There were tears of joy in her eyes. He looked over at

Coach Dru and he could see that he was crying. Little Dru was running around the court high-fiving people.

LeBron looked up and closed his eyes. He thought about Coach Kelker, the Walkers, Coach Dru, Maverick Carter, and all of the people who had helped him along the way. He remembered the people who had believed in him and who had made him believe in himself.

Life could be hard and it could be filled with uncertainty and a thousand things that could pull you down. But LeBron had also discovered that the world was filled with good people and family just waiting to happen. All you had to do was roll with it.

Life was good.

And it could only get better.

Full Circle

Life did get even better for LeBron.

He was named Ohio Mr. Basketball for the third consecutive year, the only high school player in Ohio to receive that honor. After graduating from St. V in 2003, he signed a $90 million endorsement contract with Nike and was then taken in the first round of the NBA draft by the Cleveland Cavaliers.

In his first year in the NBA, LeBron was named Rookie of the Year. From there he went on to become the youngest player in NBA history to reach 10,000 points. He won two MVP awards with the Cavaliers, before deciding to leave for the Miami Heat in 2010. While playing for the Heat, he won two more MVP awards and picked up two NBA championship rings along the way. LeBron also received two gold medals for playing on the USA Olympic basketball team in 2008 and 2012.

Despite two NBA championships with the Miami Heat, LeBron kept feeling that there was something missing. That something was Akron, the place where he had grown up and a place where he wanted his children to grow up. On July 11, 2014, LeBron announced that he was leaving the Miami Heat to play for the Cleveland Cavaliers again.

He told *Sports Illustrated* simply, "I'm coming home."

And he did.

Nine days after making the announcement of his homecoming, LeBron was sitting in a blue folding chair in a gym in Lexington, Kentucky.

He wasn't an international basketball superstar today; instead he was just a proud dad watching another LeBron playing for the Northeast Ohio Shooting Stars at an Under-11 AAU national tournament game.

He was shouting instructions to LeBron James, Jr. and his son was taking it all in.

During the next play, a teammate fed LeBron Jr. the ball. He spotted the open lane and drove to the basket and made a pretty layup. LeBron Sr. went wild. He stood up and cheered loudly, stamping his feet, clapping his hands, and calling out.

He sat back down and closed his eyes. He thought about his mom. When he was chosen for the first time to be the NBA MVP he said to her in his speech: "I still don't know how you did it." He meant how she managed to hold herself and LeBron together, despite all the challenges faced by a teenage single mother. His heart was full of gratitude to his mother and to the others who had helped him along the way. And now he was able to give so much to his children and to other children through his LeBron James Family Foundation. Everything had come full circle. His heart had led him straight back to where he had started. Back to Akron where he belonged.

He watched his son moving quickly and

effortlessly on the court and started remembering all the good times he had with the Fab Four when he was about his son's age. LeBron was lost in thought when the buzzer for the end of the game sounded. He stood up and walked over to his son. He grabbed him, went down to the floor, and started rolling around with him on the court. The entire Shooting Stars team then dog-piled on top of him.

LeBron was smiling so hard he thought his face might break.

Great reads from Sole Books!

The Flea – The Amazing Story of Leo Messi by Michael Part

Crisitano Ronaldo – The Rise of a Winner by Michael Part

Neymar The Wizard by Michael Part

The Pope Who Loves Soccer by Michael Part

The Wild Soccer Bunch series by Joachim Masannek

I Love Soccer – Featuring Landon Donovan by Stephen Berg

Baby's First Soccer by Stephen Berg

The World's Best Soccer Strikers by Noah Davis

www.solebooks.com

www.wildsoccer.com

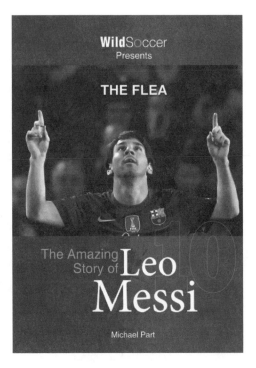

The Flea - The Amazing Story of Leo Messi

By Michael Part

The captivating story of soccer legend Lionel Messi, from his first touch at age five in the streets of Rosario, Argentina, to his first goal on the Camp Nou pitch in Barcelona, Spain. *The Flea* tells the amazing story of a boy who was born to play the beautiful game and destined to become the world's greatest soccer player. The best-selling book by Michael Part is a must read for every soccer fan!

Ages 9 and up